Irish Renaissance Annual III

Editorial Board

General Editor   Zack Bowen
Managing Editor   Dennis Jackson
Editors   James Carens
    Daniel Casey
    Patrick McCarthy
    George Mills Harper
    Barton R. Friedman
    William Murphy
    Bernard Benstock
    Emmet Larkin
Editorial Associates   Raymond Callahan
    Bonnie Scott
Associate Managing Editors   Lindsey Tucker
    Fleda Jackson
Editorial Assistant   Derek vanBever

Manuscripts submitted should follow the University of Chicago *Manual of Style* in form and documentation. We expect that the *Irish Renaissance Annual* will appear every year in the spring. Contributions and inquiries should be addressed to Zack Bowen, the *Irish Renaissance Annual,* Department of English, University of Delaware, Newark, DE 19711.

The *Irish Renaissance Annual* is published by the University of Delaware Press through Associated University Presses.

Irish Renaissance Annual III

Edited by Dennis Jackson

Newark
University of Delaware Press
London and Toronto: Associated University Presses

© 1982 by Associated University Presses, Inc.

Associated University Presses, Inc.
4 Cornwall Drive
East Brunswick, N.J. 08816

Associated University Presses Ltd
27 Chancery Lane
London WC2A 1NS, England

Associated University Presses
Toronto M5E 1A7, Canada

ISSN 0-193-9777
ISBN 0-87413-213-4
1982
(Volume III)

Printed in the United States of America

Contents

Notes on Contributors	7
Editor's Foreword	9
A Flann for All Seasons *Bernard Benstock*	15
Flann O'Brien's Timefoolery *Richard F. Peterson*	30
Waking the Dead: *The Islandman* and the Irish Revival *John Wilson Foster*	47
Austin Clarke: The Poet's Image of Frustrated Love *Beth Timson*	59
Yeats's Apocalyptic Horsemen *Edward Hirsch*	71
Maud Gonne MacBride: Violent Pacifist *Conrad A. Balliet*	93
The Presence of Parnell in Three Plays by Lady Gregory *Benilde Montgomery*	106
French Reporter Visits Volunteers' Training Camp *Simone Téry, Translated by Marilyn Gaddis Rose*	124
Irish Censorship and "The Pleasure of the Text": The "Aeolus" Episode of Joyce's *Ulysses* *Cheryl Herr*	141

Notes on Contributors

CONRAD A. BALLIET is Professor of English at Wittenberg University. His numerous articles have appeared in *PMLA, Victorian Poetry, College English, Research Studies, Notes and Queries*, the *Bulletin of the New York Public Libraries*, the *Journal of Irish Literature, Modern British Literature, MOSAIC*, and *Éire-Ireland*.

BERNARD BENSTOCK is Professor of English and Comparative Literature at the University of Illinois at Urbana-Champaign. Articles and reviews on Flann O'Brien have appeared in *Bucknell Review, Éire-Ireland, Comparative Literature Studies, New Boston Review*, and the *A.C.I.S. Newsletter*, and the entry on Flann is forthcoming in the *Encyclopedia of World Literature in the 20th Century* to be published by Frederick Ungar. His most recent book is *Who's He When He's at Home: A James Joyce Directory* (with Shari Benstock).

JOHN WILSON FOSTER is presently Associate Professor of English at the University of British Columbia. He is author of *Forces and Themes in Ulster Fiction* (1974) and of numerous articles on folklore, eighteenth-century poetry and Irish literature.

CHERYL HERR is Assistant Professor of English at Virginia Polytechnic Institute and State University. She has published pieces on Joyce in the *James Joyce Quarterly* and the *Wake Newslitter*, and is currently writing a book on *Ulysses* and Irish mass culture.

EDWARD HIRSCH teaches in the English Department at Wayne State University. He has published articles on Yeats in

ELH, The Journal of the Folklore Institute, and *Genre.* He also has a book of poems, *For the Sleepwalkers,* published by Alfred A. Knopf (May 1981).

BENILDE MONTGOMERY is a member of the Franciscan Brothers, Brooklyn Congregation. He is on the faculty of St. Joseph's College in Patchogue, New York. His publications include articles in the *Anglo-Welsh Review,* the *American Academy of Religion,* and *Renascence.*

RICHARD F. PETERSON is Professor of English at Southern Illinois University at Carbondale. He is the author of the Twayne book *Mary Lavin.* His writings on modern Irish writers have appeared in *Modern Fiction Studies, Studies in Short Fiction,* the *James Joyce Quarterly, Éire-Ireland, The Journal of Irish Literature,* and *The Sean O'Casey Review.* His book on W. B. Yeats is scheduled for publication by Twayne in 1982.

MARILYN GADDIS ROSE is founder and director of the SUNY-Binghamton translator training program, and editor of *Translation Spectrum: Essays in Theory and Practice* (SUNY Press, 1981) as well as earlier anthologies *Translation in the Humanities, Translation: Agent of Communication (Pacific Quarterly* monograph), and *Style in Translation* (Paintbrush monograph issue). She has published monographs on *Jack B. Yeats: Painter and Poet* and *Katharine Tynan Hinkson.*

BETH TIMSON is a Lecturer in the English Department at the University of North Carolina at Charlotte. She is coauthor of *Making a Difference* (a textbook on women in U.S. history) and author of articles in *Postscript* and the *Journal of Popular Culture.*

Editor's Foreword

Irish Renaissance Annual III is a general issue treating eight modern Irish writers from three points of view: their artistic achievement, their use of source material and literary antecedents, and their relation to the politics of Ireland during the past century.

In "A Flann for All Seasons," the first of two essays on the modern Irish writer Flann O'Brien, Bernard Benstock provides an overview of the O'Brien canon, taking the position that the writer's powers were in decline in works following *The Hard Life*, and arguing against the claims of "resurrectionists" who sought to sustain the earned reputation of O'Brien's earlier career by explaining away the well-worn patterns into which his later work falls. Benstock traces the parody forms of the "Cyclops," "Nausicaa," and "Oxen of the Sun" episodes of *Ulysses*, by way of contrast with the parodies in *At Swim-Two-Birds*, concluding that "what evolves as 'good' literature in *At Swim-Two-Birds* is the sum of the parts. The uneven quality in various excerpts and the thinness of the frame are compensated for by the novel as a whole, as a parody of the creative process and even a mordant statement about the state of the Irish novel, Circa 1939."

Richard F. Peterson in "Flann O'Brien's Timefoolery" examines the author's burlesquing of the ways in which devices such as time were employed by both scientist and artist. Peterson details the methods by which time parodies are developed in *The Dalkey Archive* and *At Swim-Two-Birds*.

In the first of the next three papers, which deal with artistic antecedents and the evaluation of the place of the writers' careers in Irish intellectual history, John Wilson Foster in

"Waking the Dead: *The Islandman* and the Irish Revival" makes a powerful case for Tomás Ó Crohan's *The Islandman* as a peasant experience of the revival based on history (folktales, lore), present action (his own biography), and fiction. Foster sees Ó Crohan's novel as a precursor of Joyce's *Portrait* and of Gabriel Conroy's Easterner-Dubliner figure in "The Dead." Foster claims Ó Crohan is writing a "first" novel, like Defoe making a primitive beginning and, in effect, rediscovering the genre two hundred years after Defoe. Further, Foster claims that this late artistic development is an accurate parallel of the intellectual progress of a group of people (the Blasket Islanders) who are about two hundred years behind in technological development, but who rekindle the freshness of an earlier age and form some of the intellectual roots upon which Gabriel Conroy draws.

In "Austin Clarke: The Poet's Image of Frustrated Love," Beth Timson's thesis is that the major theme of Clarke's work from his early poetry, based upon medieval and Irish Renaissance poetry, to his later, more realistic, shorter works, is that impersonal forces, namely the church, have denied physical or romantic love to the Irish. Timson's article gives a previously unexplored focus to the long career of this respected Irish poet.

Edward Hirsch's "Yeats's Apocalyptic Horsemen," the last in a series of papers dealing with source material, is one of two papers involving Yeats in the current issue. Hirsch offers a detailed explanation of Yeats's sources for the Daughters of Herodias, whose striking image dominates poem six of "Nineteen Hundred and Nineteen." He traces their origins through the history of the Sidhe and other temptress archetypes to bring new light and meaning to this important Yeats poem.

The rest of this third volume of the *Irish Renaissance Annual* is devoted to articles dealing with literature and politics. The first, Conrad Balliet's "Maud Gonne MacBride: Violent Pacifist," documents the two antagonistic forces which pulled the tempestuous and colorful actress: her fierce patriotism and her abhorrence for violence, which coexist in her speeches, her letters, and her public writing. Balliet also uses Yeats quotations in his description of her dual nature, one in which pacificism must take second place to nationalistic zeal.

Benilde Montgomery's "The Presence of Parnell in Three Plays by Lady Gregory" indicates how Lady Gregory's well-known rebel nationalism was shaped by her devotion to the Chief, while noting the fact that Parnell is treated at any length in only three of her plays and is only once alluded to by name. It is in *The Deliverer*, Montgomery suggests, that the Parnell-Moses correspondences are most apparent; the later *Dervorgilla* has its parallels to Parnell's career in its treatment of adultery and in its political history; and *Grania* similarly includes correspondences in the lack of forgiveness of the Irish mob and in its stress upon the fatalistic and tragic as well as upon the theme of resurrection associated with Parnell.

Marilyn Gaddis Rose's translation of Simone Téry's "French Reporter Visits Volunteers' Training Camp" is not necessarily literature as it was known in the period of the Irish Renaissance, but a factual report that often reads like a short story or like the new fact-fiction novels of the sixties and seventies. It provides a fresh view of an era not yet dead, as Téry's heavy use of dialogue creates an almost fictive situation. The work, though intended for publication in French newspapers as a contemporary assessment of the Black and Tan Wars, is really a romantic portrait of the popular hero General Michael Brennan. In its attention less to detail than to the essence of her visit, Téry's account is the first of a kind of new creative journalism with less emphasis upon fact than on the flavor of a heroic but miniature army fighting a guerrilla war in the 1920s.

The last essay in the current issue, Cheryl Herr's "Irish Censorship and 'The Pleasure of the Text': The 'Aeolus' Episode of Joyce's *Ulysses*," treats the nature and extent of censorship in Ireland in the late nineteenth and early twentieth centuries and relates it to the "Aeolus" episode, which comments on the role of the artist in Ireland. Herr reviews

Joyce's theme of artist and politics and treats extensively its historical and political backgrounds. This most revealing and informative essay sheds new light on the meaning of both the episode and the novel as a whole.

The *Irish Renaissance Annual* seeks to provide a forum for papers dealing with late-nineteenth and twentieth-century Irish literature. Manuscripts may be submitted to Zack Bowen, General Editor, *Irish Renaissance Annual,* Department of English, University of Delaware, Newark, DE 19711.

Zack Bowen, General Editor

Irish
Renaissance Annual
III

A Flann for All Seasons
By Bernard Benstock

In spring a young man's fancy likely turns to thoughts of indolence, but Flann O'Brien's young student-hero in *At Swim-Two-Birds* carries his predilection for his bed through a full cycle of the seasons. The author's own youth, however, was hardly misspent: *At Swim-Two-Birds* is a seasoned product of youthful enthusiasm and mature talent, and remains one of the few Irish novels that ever develops beyond Edwardian realism or Zolaesque naturalism, especially for a homegrown commodity. Youth proved shortlived for Flann O'Brien; the luxury of having three lives simultaneously depleted rather than augmented his energies, and his summer quickly burned dry, propelling him prematurely into the winter of his discontent.

That his crazyquilted literary career paralleled his frustrated life compounds the pathetic situation, yet many a reader of Irish literature must have breathed a sigh of relief when it became apparent that the intricacies and vagaries of *At Swim* were abandoned for the comic fantasies of the later novels. The post-*Swim* emphasis in Flann/Myles returned those readers to familiar ground, whose signposts are well charted within the Irish comic tradition. Few would agree with me that *At Swim-Two-Birds* stands as a landmark in imaginative literary creation rarely attempted again by any Irish novelist, not even the surviving Flann O'Brien. *The Hard Life*, following hard upon *At Swim*, represents a serious regression and a pathetic compromise; what follows thereafter is compounded pathos coupled with chaos and confusion. And only the author's untimely and undignified death arrested the rocky downhill slide. The Burkes and Hares of literary criticism took possession of the corpse and the corpus, and went to work establishing Flann O'Brien's reputation at the level they preferred.

It was easier for the Resurrectionionists to explain away a single aberrant item like *At Swim* than have to face the general loss of ambitious scope which marks the ensuing works, and as William Faulkner indicated when evaluating the best American novelists of his own generation, it is the *ambition* of the undertaking that is the most significant element in estimating a literary career. The essential talents remained despite disappointment and anxieties, but they were channeled along a series of relatively familiar grooves: the wildly comic, the agony of despair, the pretension to indifference that underlines an acceptance of futility, the lugubrious dark that nonetheless hints at religious miracle, and the skillful blend of these diverse factors into near-plausible fantasy. We pick our way through the jerry-built and gerrymandered O'Brien canon, finding many delightful moments at which these components are at their best and something innate in the Flann O'Brien talent is perceivable. But never again are we exposed to the ingenuities and innovations that characterize *At Swim-Two-Birds*.

As is the case with most over-ambitious ventures, the chances for total success are slim, but the nature of the attempt explains and compensates for the failures. In *At Swim-Two-Birds* Flann O'Brien searches for a governing structure that will support a necessarily diverse panoply, while constantly suggesting that all structures are artificial and doomed to destruction. In effect he began with the destructive element, attacking the monochromatic and linear plot progression characteristic of the traditional novel. "One beginning and one ending for a book was a thing I did not agree with," states O'Brien's tentative artist-as-a-young-man with syntactical simplicity and glittering ingenuity; "A good book may have three openings entirely dissimilar and interrelated only in the prescience of the author, or for that matter one hundred times as many endings."[1] (That the goal of such experimentation is the ideal "good book" gets quietly buried among the audacities, but it must be eventually resurrected as central to O'Brien's scheme in *At Swim*.)

For the premise challenged (the single vein of plot line) two species are presented: a workable but presumably arbitrary set of *three*, and an exaggerative and presumably unworkable hundred—actually three hundred. The nature of the exaggeration for hyperbolic emphasis is exposed in the construction which allows for a hundred different endings for each of the three openings. The trinitarian structure is hardly accidental: we need no Saint Patrick waving a shamrock under our noses to accept the traditional values of a trinity that remains and characterizes an essential unity. The chaos conjured up by the threat of vague hundreds is calmed by the assurance of a familiar three, and life parallels art from the opening sentence to assure us that the pattern is an intended and fixed one ("Having placed in my mouth sufficient bread for three minutes' chewing . . . " [9].) Casually and almost halfheartedly the three openings are advanced (the first on the Pooka, the second on John Furriskey, and the third on Finn MacCool), yet the neat compartmentalization is immediately discernible as a patent fraud: Flann O'Brien's novel had already begun prior to these three openings with a narrator chewing bread, and thereafter continues with his hurting a tooth on a "lump of the crust" (10). Hard reality—in the shape of a crust of basic bread—intrudes into the trinitarian fantasy and persists throughout the book. As soon as the essential One is sub-divided into a tight triangle of three, a back door has been opened unto the fourth (akin to the Irish folk-Trinity of the Father and the Son and the Holy Ghost and the Banshee).

Accepting the fiction of the fiction, a young novelist lying in bed writing a book which has three openings because he is juggling a trio of characters (and their individual plot lines leading toward inter-relationship), we willingly suspend disbelief to allow for the squared triangle and naively assume that we have reached a finite stasis. What we have failed to allow for are two vastly disturbing elements: the erratic ineptness of the young novelist that makes his manuscript problematical, and the persistence of external forces at work on his physical being, so that despite his tenacious retreat to his bedroom, there is no guarantee of uninterrupted progress on the novel. O'Brien presents not only the creative product (in bits and pieces) but also a parody of the creative process. The neophyte at work begins by pontificating on critical theory ("A good book may have . . . "), immediately showing his hand and giving the game away, and he continues to display his inexperience by interrupting the narrative flow—of his exposed "autobiography" as well as his proposed "book"—by stating his intentions *("Description of my uncle . . . Quality of rasher in use in household . . . Nature of denial" [11–13]*). Such textbook categorization reveals the skeletal structure and soon displaces the flesh itself. These internal interruptions are paralleled by external ones: mail from a horse-betting tout, visits by his uncle despite the presumably locked door of the bedroom, more welcome visits from Brinsley which are distractions nonetheless, and the basic failure of dogged consistency as he finds it necessary to break his hibernative pattern to occasionally attend the university and embark on an embryonic drinking career in the pubs. "Real life," a spectre he somehow hopes to capture in his art, captures him instead, rising above his aspirations to become the *real* novelist's captive, the achievement of Flann O'Brien. The anonymous writer, generously involved in the process of *naming* all of his own characters and alive amid a host of named people, but deprived by his creator of a name of his own, hiccoughs his way through his creativity with inartistic self-interruptions until he has so exhausted himself as to have to offer his prospective reader a synopsis of what has gone before. And the synoptic itself can become habit-forming: "Before proceeding further, the Reader is respectfully advised to refer to the Synopsis or Summary of the Argument on Page 85" (145).

The efforts of the narrator to contain himself in an egocentric universe, and thus contain his fictional characters in a finite universe, are doomed by the nature of diversity, parturition and anastomosis. Once the One has begun to subdivide, the possible spinoffs are infinite. The Pooka *engenders* the Good Fairy; John Furriskey *owes his existence* to Dermot Trellis; Finn MacCool *requires* an audience and interlocutors for his endless stream of voluntary expostulation and reluctant revelations. The young novelist who saw himself as their creator—and the only necessary creator—can neither control the mushrooming process of creation nor keep the creative formula secreted in his hermetically sealed bedroom. As a First Number he requires, without ever admitting the necessity, his own creator, a Previous Number. He may conveniently have no visible parents anywhere about, but is nonetheless somewhat dependent upon a residual and persistent Uncle who feels himself to be responsible for him. His dependent position is an embarrassment and an inconvenience, but it proves inevitable: he is even pressed into service as secretary for his uncle's committee, as humiliating for the creative *writer* as being a Civil Servant must have been to Flann O'Brien.

"For all proper things do stand out distinct from one another" (8) reads the writing on the wall (and the epigraph in Greek prefixed to *At Swim-Two-Birds*), but in his Platonic cave the tyro novelist cannot see the graffito. Just as he fails to contain his characters (they multiply almost at will), he is also unable to discern their distinctiveness. On one hand, by a process akin to spontaneous combustion, the Jem Caseys and mad Sweenys appear—and surely each of them deserves an opening of his own—while on the other, by a process akin to superfetation, all of Dermot Trellis's additional characters take shape. By creating Furriskey on the first page, hasn't the student-novelist leapfrogged the "author" who has given birth to the Furriskey character? And just as Dermot Trellis can beget the son Orlick who will also write a book and attempt to write his father out of it, so does the established writer require a predecessor in William Tracy, who has originally (one supposes) created the characters that Trellis commandeers and absorbs into his own book. Tracy begets Trellis who begets Orlick; the narrator creates Trellis who creates Furriskey, Shanahan, and Lamont (and incorporates Slug and Shorty); Flann engenders the narrator who in turn engenders all of his fictional personages. The ensuing progress backward and outward continues the process.

Against this expansive burgeoning toward infinity and the threatening population explosion within the novelist's universe, the only potent force in action is the narrator's attempts to delimit by number. The Pooka and the Good Fairy develop a numerological tension between odd and even numbers in their game of one-upmanship, but this too leads into dangerous multiplications. In opposition to the engulfing hundreds the narrator insists on the basic three, his number for stability and total containment. But it is an uphill fight to sustain his three-pronged opening against the onslaught of hundreds of endings. His triangularization of the target results in the first significantly negative criticism of his manuscript when Brinsley gratuitously maintains that there is little to distinguish in the characterizations of Furriskey, Shanahan, and Lamont: "The three of them, he said, might make one man between them" (230). This anti-Trinitarian heresy unnerves the fledgling novelist who declares his trio to be "profoundly dissimilar" (231). His *Memorandum of the respective diacritical traits or qualities of Messrs. Furriskey, Lamont and Shanahan*" (231) differentiates along the most superficial lines—physical description, clothing, mannerisms, and even favorite flowers, shrubs and dishes. As Flann O'Brien's exercise in comic cataloguing, the list is an inspired one of "words which I rarely used" (231) (what Stephen Dedalus would recognize as "literary" language[2]), but as aspects of distinction to satisfy the Greek spirit, they prove meaningless. The assumption is that in delineating character any three different traits are distinctive factors, so that brachycephalic, bullet, and prognathic head shapes could hardly be mistaken for each other. But character depends on *intrinsic* features, and nothing enumerated in the Memorandum individualizes any of the three. Of what significance is it that Furriskey's nose is roman, while Lamont's is snub, and Shanahan's is mastoid? And in a series of triangles, what happens to a particular figurative pattern when one of the angles is missing (for pedal traits Lamont is nil, for volar traits Shanahan is nil)?

This failure to distinguish one thing from another, to separate the three persons of his Trinity from each other, loses the novelist his best friend and severest critic. As an ally against the Philistine Uncle, friend Brinsley proves all too accommodating, diplomatically siding with the uncle as a gesture to disarm him and aid the nephew by mollifying the adversary. The uncle, however, takes Brinsley at his word and they march off together, leaving the writer alone and deserted. The one person who has actually been privy to part of the manuscript has been negative in his criticism, has been ineffectually resisted when his criticism proved too discomforting, and has been subsequently lost. By contrast, the novelist's most gratifying admirer is someone who hasn't seen a word of the book-in-progress, the guru Michael Byrne, who has no qualms about excessively admiring a piece of work he has not read. It is the negative instance of the work of literature that affords the writer his finest praise.

Not that anyone should have expected that the anonymous student-author would produce a literary masterpiece. In effect, his "novel" disintegrates before the reader's eyes: portions are lost, gaps have to be repeatedly summarized, serious flaws emerge and are pinpointed (much to the author's chagrin), and the threat of incendiary disappearance hovers over the entire project. Our author is hardly immune to the calamity that befell Thomas Carlyle and Dermot Trellis, but even more threatening than having a manuscript go up in smoke is having his story go up in air. After all, it is *talking about* his novel that proves far more successful than committing it to paper (Michael Byrne proving more receptive than Brinsley), and it is many a good Irish writer's fate to enjoy his creativity in the social atmosphere of good talk. Nor should we make the obvious mistake of assuming that the bedprone novelist has actually delivered himself of several "excerpts" from a work in progress. It is no more valid to credit him with Flann O'Brien's excerpts than to credit the anonymous collector of bad debts in the "Cyclops" portion of *Ulysses* with James Joyce's intrusions of giganticism.

The structure of *At Swim-Two-Birds* depends upon that basic premise that an indolent and inexpert Irish writer (youth remains his ingratiating excuse) attempts against impossible odds to write a modern Irish novel. The impossibility is built into the Irish literary tradition, a history of ancient writings in Gaelic, a facile tendency in the oral heritage, a conflicting preponderance of folkloristic material, a "poetic" capacity that often overflows the vessel that is intended to contain it, a talent for mimicry that can easily subsume the necessity of creating an original voice—all of which is in constant conflict with the disheartening realities of Irish life (Stephen Dedalus writing his exotic villanelle in his grim bedroom). The protagonist's reward at the end of *At Swim* is neither publication nor even a completed manuscript, but a secondhand watch and a begrudging acknowledgment from his uncle of his success as a university student. Flann O'Brien had no more intention of sharing his success as an author with his young artist than did James Joyce, and his repeated disdain for his completed and published first novel attests to the tortured psychology of his relationship with his own masterpiece.

That "good book" envisioned by the potential novelist at the opening of *At Swim-Two-Birds* remains a modest ideal for both him and his immediate superior. Two factors, however, stood solidly and discouragingly in the way of the good new novelist circa 1939: the enormous accomplishment of Irish novelist James Joyce and the vociferous and often conflicting demands of Ireland itself on its artists. In his initial novel Flann O'Brien sought to confront both these spectres, although there is no ignoring his displeasure with the assignment. The nature of the innovations in *Ulysses* precluded the possibility of *At Swim* emerging as a traditional novel, and the context of the "Cyclops" chapter in particular may have been instrumental in determining the specifically Irish parodies present in Flann O'Brien's creation. Flann's Finn grumbles that "Finn is without honour in the breast of a sea-blue book" (24), perhaps a hint that O'Brien saw the possibilities of utilizing the Finn MacCool legend for parodic purposes since Joyce had done nothing with it (he had no way of knowing the title of Joyce's next book, since it was kept secret even from the publisher of *Finnegans Wake* until the last minute). In taking for himself a healthy measure of specifically Irish material, Flann O'Brien could effectively leapfrog over Joyce's eschewing of that area and also satisfy a national demand for new Irish literature based on basic Irish themes.

Yet Joyce's penchant for parody hilariously colors Flann's treatment of those Irish elements. Parody is a safe position for the author: it neither commits him to accept or treat his raw materials with total seriousness nor prevents him from deriving maximum credit for their incorporation. That the fledgling writer can start his three hares simultaneously distances Finn, Furriskey, and the Pooka (legend, fiction, and folklore) from Flann himself. He is not responsible for the faults of his fledgling but can nonetheless claim the credit from the ribald comedy engendered by the unique characterization of the latterday Finn.

Anne Clissmann notes "some thirty-six different styles and forty-two extracts"[3] in *At Swim-Two-Birds,* and unless someone bothers to build a better computer, these seem satisfactory numbers for anyone's purpose. The scope is certainly extensive, from the antics of Finn and King Sweeny to the Dublin cowboys Slug and Shorty, from moralistic tracts posing as fiction to pick-and-shovel panegyrics posing as poetry. It is the imaginative sweep of the varieties of parodic experience that gives *At Swim* its sustaining power despite the fragile frame upon which Flann stretches his audacities. Nevertheless, Joyce's art of parody looms behind at all times, establishing the mode which Flann O'Brien subsumes and attempts to circumvent. There are, of course, important differences in their handling of the parodic mode, as well as a significant distinction in the placement of parody within the particular novel. Joyce's *Ulysses* incorporates parody partially in two chapters, "Cyclops" and "Nausicaa," and exclusively in a third, "Oxen of the Sun," while *At Swim* depends almost entirely on the success of a diverse series of parodies throughout. It is in "Cyclops" that Joyce deploys his pieces of parody in a manner similar to Flann O'Brien's.

"Cyclops" depends upon its realistic situation, the confrontation of the pacifistic but cornered Leopold Bloom with the aggressively xenophobic Citizen; the manner of presentation is to "allow" a feisty pubsprawler as sole narrative voice and arbiter of tone; the confrontation builds within the confines of a flow of pub talk, all of which is heightened and augmented by interpolated parodies of literary and quasi-literary styles (twenty-eight of them, if anyone is counting, although some are merely fragments while others are fairly elaborate and extensive). The reader can easily segregate the intrusions from the narrative flow within guideposts, primarily because of the distinctiveness of the narrator's gab and the sharpness of the parodic pieces. Yet two of the presiding voices, the narrator's and the Citizen's, are in themselves of such quaint eloquence that they occasionally rise to the occasion and in human terms approximate gigantic exaggeration. Despite the purposeful intrusions, the chapter retains its integrity and wholeness, and the portions of giganticism contribute to advancing the plot of *Ulysses*.

The plot of *At Swim-Two-Birds*, on the other hand, is intentionally skimpy: Vivian Mercier classifies it as an anti-novel, and Anne Clissmann seconds the notion. The inverse pyramid builds the parodies upward into the major proportions of the novel balanced on the excuse of the indolent literateur at work while he wards off the few realities of his existence (the intruding uncle, the university, the experience of learning to drink bottled stout). The "extracts" from the typescript are worked off against the "biographical reminiscences" so that it becomes apparent that they are equally fictional formats, the novelist/biographer at work against himself. Unity of form is hardly the intention here; it is orchestrated chaos that forms the structural intentions of *At Swim-Two-Birds*. What becomes obvious is that Finn Mac-Cool can only exist in the breast of a sea-blue book, a figurative construction that is at once gigantic enough to have "three fifties of fosterlings . . . engage with handball against the wideness of his backside" (10) and still sit within the room at the Red Swan, a superannuated bore endlessly babbling of green fields. Joyce's Citizen, however, very much a counterpart to the Finn who is described as "not mentally robust, [but] . . . a man of superb physique" (10), retains his real existence (both in his prototype, Michael Cusack, and in his fictional reality in the licensed premises of Bernard Kiernan's), despite momentary lapses in which he expands into a "broadshouldered deepchested stronglimbed frankeyed redhaired freely freckled shaggybearded widemouthed largenosed longheaded deepvoiced barekneed brawnyhanded hairylegged ruddyfaced sinewyarmed hero."[4] A caricature of Finn and a dropsical pub fixture, he is augmented and deflated by the satiric thrusts of the narrative, yet oddly enough he has his one moment of inflated glory, rising to genuine heights of heroism in his rhetorical plaint on the destruction of Ireland's greatness. Parody and pathos are suspended for his insightful analysis of the present plight of Ireland which begins, "Where are our missing twenty millions of Irish should be here today instead of four, our lost tribes?"[5] Amidst the pastiches of legal briefs, social notes, catalogues of heroes, epic descriptions, and journalistic and medical reports, his single speech stands out as true eloquence.

The two other chapters in *Ulysses* of sustained parody are also distinct from each other, and "Nausicaa" in particular deserves further comparison with *At Swim-Two-Birds*. The chapter divides into two discrete segments, a newly introduced narrative voice that derives from sentimental Victorian fiction for young girls and a complementary interior monologue along familiar lines of Bloom's masculine-sentimental thoughts. Parody is clearly played off against mundane reality, but it is a consistent parodic mode which develops a total pattern of its own, sets the scene, establishes the dramatis personae, presents a decided point of view, and lampoons itself in the process, all the while keeping the central focus of the Bloom story in the forefront. The dissociation which separates the student-author from his fictional creations is absent from "Nausicaa," and Joyce's art of parody once again proves to be a cohesive rather than divisive factor in the narrative. Gerty MacDowell's perspective, transmitted with uncanny faithfulness by a hilarious narrative device, coincides perfectly with Bloom's self-effacing romanticism: as the opening technique moves Bloom ineluctably into the web of Gerty's imagined desires, the contrasting view of Bloom's thoughts reveals the impossibility of his giving himself up to any precarious relationship, despite his overwhelming passions, and he retreats into further loneliness and compensating onanism. The movement toward and away, developed by the dual techniques of parody and interior monologue, provides rhythmic flow and conceptual balance. By contrast, Flann O'Brien's piecemeal alternations of outlandish parody and gentle spoof (the "extracts" and the "reminiscences"), accomplished as they are and magnificently comic at times, are hardly intended for the poignant resolution with which "Nausicaa" closes.

The major contrast of the deployment of parody is between "Oxen of the Sun" and *At Swim-Two-Birds*. The basis of comparison is particularly valid since Joyce undertook to track the nine-hundred-year development of English literary prose style while O'Brien ranged far and frantically to incorporate aspects of the oral and written literary traditions of Ireland. Joyce limited himself to straight chronology, made the technique the exclusive format of the chapter, carefully provided pastiches that were committed particularly to accuracy rather than comic exaggeration, and kept the events of the narrative moving through the difficult terrain to advance the plot of the novel. O'Brien worked for diversity (where Joyce concentrated on unity), preferring comic juxtaposition, absurd interlacings, and unexpected intrusions; the result of his fanciful manipulations of interacting plots was to allow the novel-within-the-novel to gain dominance over the less significant frame story. Joyce could easily distance himself as parodist from the English prose being parodied, restraining any prejudice against the literature of the conquerors by a genuine admiration for so sophisticated a literary development. O'Brien, on the other hand, was integrally involved in the controversies on his native land, in the Gaelic language movements, in the rewriting of literary history for national esteem, and in the internecine battle which meant that whatever was gained by glorification of one aspect of the nation's literature was lost by the denigration of another. His method, therefore, was necessarily non-chronological and his examples extreme. Yet just as Joyce culminated his parodic process with the vivid but vernacular explosion of language in the drunken conclusion of "Oxen of the Sun," so did O'Brien move toward eventual diminution: Finn's mock-epic voice and the poetics of mad Sweeny give way to Jem Casey's proletarian doggerel and the Ringsend cowboy raid—the last finally reduced to a newspaper account of street rowdyism and a couple of smashed tram windows. Comic reduction certainly is the result of both experiments in literary parody, but O'Brien's purpose seems to range more widely toward every sort of diminution, from the destruction of the manuscript to the humiliating "success" of the university student.

Few readers of *Ulysses* can stomach "Oxen of the Sun," and even devoted Joyceans who can swallow it have difficulty digesting it. Yet none can deny that the parodic method is consistent and sustained, in sharp contrast with the complementary efforts in "Cyclops" to intertwine diverse types and styles. Joyce seems genuinely to have admired the fine stylistic touches of the English writers and his parody is respectful while poking gentle fun; by contrast his parodies in "Cyclops" are devastating, although he allows that even within the most crass and commercial forms of literary output a commendable flare and flourish will at times burst forth. Joyce's art of parody was founded on a fundamental delight with all aspects of literary language; Flann O'Brien's attitude was conditioned by ambivalence, a set of conflicting motivations, but his art was polished by a similar gusto and abandon that permitted him to mimic skillfully and carry mimicry into masterful absurdity. Whereas Joyce, the presumed coterie artist, retained an attitude of acceptance, finding felicities as well as falsities in both "literary" language and language "of the marketplace,"[6] O'Brien dedicated himself to separating good literature from bad.

O'Brien's parodies then are designed to deflate pompous postulations and undermine the mindlessness of simplified art. There is an uneven quality, however, in his pastiches: depicting Finn as a grumpy bore may preclude having his storytelling accepted as superior art. What does the reader do with the long Sweeny extracts which are, after all, Flann O'Brien's competent translations from the original? The short "poems" of Jem Casey are redeemed by their brevity, by the skillful way they are introduced and encompassed in the narrative, and by the comic handling of the colloquial, but the Sweeny excerpts are endless and repetitious. That the lean unlovely English fails to capture the poetic essentials of the Gaelic is a self-defeating factor in the parodic humor, the poem becoming progressively mired in the imitative fallacy. Nial Sheridan's blue pencil may have done the same yeoman service as Pound's on *The Waste Land,* but one moans along with Ben Jonson on the lines that remained unblotted. The *longeurs* may be a matter of defective reader response, especially of those readers who do not arrive at *At Swim-Two-Birds* with an insatiable thirst for prolonged Irishness, but they may also be the readers who best appreciate Flann's better parodies, where the area of originality is larger than the circumference of the imitation. The dialogue between the Pooka and the Good Fairy is built on a progressive principle of comic possibilities, the creation of a colloquy (itself a fine Irish art form) based on converse stichomythia: neither participant makes either a single comment or asks a single question, but each answers and adds to the compilation of subjects under discussion. Compounded non sequiturs develop which are actually exact responses to the previous compounds in logical and progressive order. That their dualistic personalities are also in inverse proportions to one another reinforces the farce until the internal contradiction of the Fairy's supposed goodness quickly falls apart at the poker game. Building less on a fixed commodity (Finn/Sweeny) but not dependent upon a fictional format totally of his own creation (the Trellis tales), O'Brien works best by sloshing old wines in new bottles.

What evolves as "good" literature in *At Swim-Two-Birds* is the sum of the parts. The uneven quality in various excerpts and the thinness of the frame are compensated for by the novel as a whole, as a parody of the creative process and even a mordant statement about the state of the Irish novel circa 1939. Rescuing his anti-hero from social failure (awarding him his degree and his uncle's blessing) also rescues the potential artist from the necessity of practicing his art. Nothing exceeds as well as qualified success, and the artist-hero disappears from *At Swim* at the penultimate instance to be replaced in the final section, *"Conclusion of the book, ultimate"* (314), by a new narrative voice, an over-voice that elevates the novel to a new plane, a narrator-without-identity that subsumes and reintegrates all previously existing elements and insists upon the last word, which for the Flann O'Brien persona prophetically says "good-bye"—and says it three times—a literary suicide.

NOTES

1. Flann O'Brien, *At Swim-Two-Birds* (New York: Pantheon Books Inc., 1939), p. 9. Subsequent references are included parenthetically in the text.
2. James Joyce, *A Portrait of the Artist as a Young Man* (New York: Viking, 1964), p. 188.
3. Anne Clissmann, *Flann O'Brien: A Critical Introduction to His Writings* (Dublin: Gill and Macmillan, 1975), p. 86.
4. James Joyce, *Ulysses* (New York: Random House, 1961), p. 296.
5. Joyce, *Ulysses*, p. 326.
6. Joyce, *Portrait*, p. 188.

Flann O'Brien's Timefoolery
By Richard F. Peterson

Though the time worlds of Flann O'Brien's Anglo-Irish novels are outrageously multidimensional, O'Brien's own attitude toward time and his use of time theories are relatively simple. His basic approach, not surprising at all in a punster, is to take modern thought on time, no matter how abstract and complex, quite literally. The effect of such a strategy is to expose the incredible and laughable gap between our common perception of time and the non-human universes concocted by scientists and artists. He also throws a barb at our pretensions and ludicrous efforts to interpret and explain these theories to each other. In his *Cruiskeen Lawn* column, O'Brien, acting through his alter ego Myles na gCopaleen, wrote that "there are less than a thousand people in the world who really understand the Einstein theory of relativity, and less than a 100 people who can discuss it intelligently."[1]

The primary source for the timefoolery in O'Brien's novels is the writing of Aldous Huxley or, more specifically, Huxley's *Point Counter Point*. Conveniently placed on the ledge of the washstand belonging to the narrator-hero of *At Swim-Two-Birds* are several of "the widely-read books of Mr. A. Huxley, the eminent English writer."[2] Though Huxley satirizes several time theories in *Point Counter Point*, his chief method of ridiculing the non-human ideas of modern thinkers is to give Mark Rampion, a Lawrentian hero appropriately marred by a pedagogical complex, the opportunity to preach on the subject. Rampion's view is that the "quantum theory, wave mechanics, relativity, and all the rest of it" are brain-tortured attempts to "get a faint notion of the universe as it would seem if looked at through non-human eyes." His complaint is that this "non-human truth" has no relevance to "ordinary human living" and distracts our attention from "human truth."[3]

Rampion's harsh judgment of modern scientific thought comes at the end of *Point Counter Point,* but Huxley's own timefoolery exposes the absurdity of time theories, both past and contemporary, throughout the novel. At one point, he uses Beatrice Gilray's act of stitching, a paradigm in itself from *The Odyssey* to *The Heart of Darkness* for the fateful movement of time, to illustrate and counterpoint two famous theories that stress time as inevitable. As Beatrice stitches and waits for Burlap's return from his Homeric and Dantesque adventures at the Tantamount party, the clock ticks and the "moving instant which, according to Sir Isaac Newton, separates the infinite past from the infinite future advanced inexorably through the dimension of time."[4] On the other hand, the motionless figure of Beatrice suggests the Aristotelian notion, the same one that thought-tormented Stephen Dedalus muddles over in the Nestor chapter of *Ulysses,* that "a little more of the possible was every instant made real; the present stood still and drew into itself the future, as a man might suck for ever at an unending piece of macaroni."[5] The inexorable tick of the Newtonian clock or the reeling in of the Aristotelian noodle brings Burlap safely home to Beatrice and inevitably leads to the bath scene, Huxley's annunciation of the triumph of hypocrisy in a world of empty-headed fools and ineffectual philosophers.

Flann O'Brien's time world is made up of characters who accept time theories as literal truths or encounter literal intrusions of "non-human truths" into their otherwise human world. Some of O'Brien's characters have no trouble at all accepting the incredible properties of either a microphysical or macroscopic universe. They live quite easily with the idea of relative or regressive time or a world of shifting molecules. Others, however, are caught between their belief in a predictable mechanical universe made up of time, space, and mass and their discovery of a nightmarish wonderland invented by science or art.

One of the most outrageous examples of an O'Brien character who accepts scientific thought as literal truth made his first appearance in print as the periphrastic Sergeant Fottrell, the archenemy of bicycles in *The Dalkey Archive*. Though he is often seen in the company of a bicycle, he refuses to get up on one because of what he mysteriously calls dangers inherent in the bicycle. During a chance meeting with Mick Shaughnessy, the Sergeant even admits that he deliberately steals bicycles or punctures their tires. When pressed to explain himself, the Sergeant calmly announces that "the Mollycule Theory is at work in the parish of Dalkey," and is doing "terrible destruction" to "half of the people."[6] According to the Sergeant, the good people of Dalkey are in imminent danger of becoming bicycles.

Sergeant Fottrell's anti-bicycle crusade has been inspired by his practical application of quantum theory to the dynamic relationship between human beings and bicycles. He tells Mick that everything is made up of "small mollycules of itself and they are flying around in concentric circles and arcs and segments and innumerable various other routes too numerous to mention collectively, never standing still or resting but spinning away and darting hither and thither and back again, all the time on the go" (*DA* 87). All this whirling, however, cancels itself out within each object, thus our limited perception of a Newtonian universe of absolute solidity and determinable shape. Unfortunately, what we fail to see is that when two objects strike each other or are brought into contact frequently over a long period of time, there is an interchange of "mollycules." It follows for the quantum-minded Sergeant that people who have spent most of their time riding bicycles have mixed up their properties with those of their bicycles and that a surprising number of Irish citizens living in the country have become half-bicycles, while their bicycles, in the words of the Sergeant, "partake serenely of humanity" (*DA* 89).

When Mick Shaughnessy protests that he has never seen anyone who looked like a bicycle, Sergeant Fottrell explains that when things have gone too far, a human-becoming-bicycle will give itself away by leaning with one elbow against a wall or by standing propped up on one foot by a path. As for a bicycle-becoming-human, the Sergeant says that it is too cunning to move about on its own, but he points out the curious phenomena of bicycles parked in a warm kitchen during a rainstorm and food crumbs scattered mysteriously about the front wheels. The moral and political implications are frightening, what with men riding ladies' bicycles and the possibility of bicycles made in Birmingham or Coventry gaining a majority of seats (the pun in O'Brien is always intended) in the government. The Sergeant even cites the dreadful case of a McDadd who murdered his neighbor and was arrested along with his bicycle. After carefully observing McDadd and the bicycle, the arresting officer, coincidentally a friend of McDadd, condemned the bicycle, which was dutifully hanged and buried in a bicycle-shaped coffin beside the murdered man.

Sergeant Fottrell's mania for stealing bicycles or puncturing their tires to save mankind is an example of what happens to a character who takes a non-human truth or scientific theory too seriously. In *The Dalkey Archive*, however, modern scientific theory on the nature of time actually intrudes itself upon the physical world of the novel. The fantastic appearances of St. Augustine and James Joyce are actual, rather than imaginary or proposed, because time, as opposed to being absolute, true, and mathematical in its recording of passing events, emerges, according to O'Brien, "as a great flat motionless sea. Time does not pass; it is we who pass."[7]

O'Brien believes that the responsibility for the concept of time as a vast, constant reality appearing to move and change only because of our limited understanding of its properties falls upon Einstein with his theory of relativity and J. W. Dunne with his serial universe. Both argued that our perception of time is dependent upon our position in the universe. Rather than accepting time as a mechanical movement,

Einstein postulated that the time of an event is relative to the movement and position of the observer and that a single event observed by two people situated at different distances will appear to occur at different times. The implication of Einstein's theory is that events relegated to the past by our mechanical sense of time are actually still happening and that, theoretically, if a person generated enough speed to move faster than light waves, he could overtake an event and seemingly reverse time. Dunne argued that the idea of duration accepts time moving along a time length. If, however, the movement along the time length is everywhere at once, then indeed time is a motionless sea—it does not pass at all. The only way, then, we can observe the duration of an event is by moving to another observation or time level. This step backwards, however, begins a process or serial of regresses in which observer after observer withdraws from time to record its passage. Thus to measure time we move to another time level which, in turn, can be measured only by moving to a third level and on and on.

O'Brien's shortcut through light waves and endless regresses is De Selby's D.M.P. Another transfer from *The Third Policeman*, De Selby claims to have mastered time: "Time has been called, an event, a repository, a continuum, an ingredient of the universe. I can suspend time, negative its apparent course" (*DA* 14). His reason for rejecting past explanations of time is his discovery that time is "a plenum, immobile, immutable, ineluctable, irrevocable, a condition of absolute stasis. Time does not pass. Change and movement may occur within time" (*DA* 17). De Selby simply does not need Einstein's relativity and Dunne's infinite regresses or any other intellectual or spatial construct of time because he has encountered and now can control what others have understood only in theory. He has no reason for spatializing time because he has experienced it as an unchanging, irresistible phenomenon.

Incredibly, De Selby has discovered true time while working on a way to destroy the world. His experiments in pneumatic chemistry have been guided by his conviction that the human race, debauched and diseased beyond recovery, deserves total extinction. Driven by this worsening corruption of God's nature, which is something of a cross between original sin and entropy, De Selby has invented a chemical compound, D.M.P., coincidentally the initials of the Dublin Metropolitan Police, that eliminates the oxygen from any given atmosphere. It is through D.M.P. that De Selby has made his startling discovery: "That a deoxygenated atmosphere cancels the apparently serial nature of time and confronts us with true time and simultaneously with all the things and creatures which time has ever contained or will contain, provided we evoke them" (*DA* 22).

The immediate narrative effect of D.M.P. is to give Mick Shaughnessy the idea of saving the world from De Selby's mad plot, thereby setting in motion a bizarre sequence of events culminating in the unnecessary theft (De Selby changes his mind) of a circular four-gallon container of the deadly compound. As time's elixir, however, D.M.P. has far-reaching implications for the theme, unity, and general madness of *The Dalkey Archive*. It exposes as the basic flaw or blind spot in time theories, the pseudo-intellectualization of time. Once intellectual constructs about relative positions and infinite regresses are removed, true time appears as an undeniable, irresistible, and immutable reality. Of course, De Selby wants to take away the air and breathe it, too. His chamber under the sea is a little bubble, even if deoxygenated, within the vast immensity of time, where De Selby can summon figures from the past for his own enlightenment. His selection of St. Augustine for the visit of Mick and Hackett is consistent with De Selby's own obsession with the divine order of the universe—he is as much a theologian as a physicist—but, as an illumination of the novel's time theme, it also brings forth the perfect philosopher. St. Augustine's famous statement on time is exactly the point O'Brien is making about pseudo-theories of time and explanations of theories—"What then is time? If no one asks me, I know; if I want to explain it to a questioner, I do not know."

This common sense approach to time would obviously

appeal to a writer disturbed by all the hot air released over the question of time. Actually, an obsession with air, which for O'Brien symbolizes an attempt to spatialize time, is the common link between the trinity of madcap timesters in *The Dalkey Archive*. Sergeant Fottrell wants to save humanity from rampaging "mollycules" by letting the air out of bicycle tires, while De Selby wants to let the air out of the atmosphere to destroy the human race. James Joyce, the last of the trinity to turn up, wants to save the Church and, in the process, the soul of mankind by letting the air out of the Holy Trinity. His plan is to eliminate the Holy Spirit because the early fathers mistakenly associated *pneuma* with the working of a hypostatic Third Person rather than as a breath of God the Father. In other words, Joyce believes the whole notion of the Holy Spirit is a case of hot air being taken as literal truth.

The incredible resurrection of James Joyce in *The Dalkey Archive* has received a great deal of critical attention, most focusing on O'Brien's own obsession with Joyce. In terms of the timefoolery in the novel, however, Joyce's appearance offers yet another variation on O'Brien's parody of time speculators. While the words and deeds of Sergeant Fottrell and De Selby mock both microphysical and macroscopic time theories, Joyce's antics call into question the efforts of historians and biographers to rearrange and even deify the life and times of their subjects. The canonization or Ellmannization of Joyce by American scholars was always a sore spot for O'Brien, and in *The Dalkey Archive*, he clearly ridicules Joyceans as he has his sport with Joyce.

The shock of what James Joyce says to Mick Shaughnessy, who wants Mary to write an unprecedented book on the "true story" of Joyce, is that it contradicts the elaborate myths invented by critics. Rather than the literary rebel proclaiming that he will not serve, O'Brien's Joyce wants to join the Jesuit Order. As for the brilliance and daring attributed to the author of *Ulysses* and *Finnegans Wake*, this Joyce denies having written either book. He denounces *Ulysses* as "pornography and filth and literary vomit" *(DA*

194) written by "muck-rakers, obscene poets, carnal pimps, sodomous sycophants, pedlars of the coloured lusts of fallen humanity" *(DA* 193) in the hire of Sylvia Beach, who loved Joyce and wanted to make him famous. As for *Finnegans Wake,* Joyce knows the ballad, but has never heard of the book.

Actually, O'Brien's parody of Joyce is based on the same Blephen characteristics that have fanned the enthusiasms of scholars. Joyce's desire "to get into the Jesuits, you might say, to clear the Holy Ghost out of the Godhead and out of the Catholic Church" *(DA* 201) is suspiciously like Stephen's interest in heretical interpretations of the Holy Trinity. Joyce's self-imposed exile as a curate in Skerries where he writes booklets for the Catholic Truth Society on the dangers of alcohol and attends daily mass has the ring of Bloom's delightful inconsistencies, while echoing Stephen's silence, exile, and cunning and his super-saturation with the Catholic Church. O'Brien's final touch is to have his Joyce insulted by Father Cobble, who wants the supplicant to join the houseboy staff so that he can be in charge of repairing the undergarments of all the Jesuit Fathers living in Dublin—a just fate for Jesuit-baiting Stephen and a merciful one for Bloom with his perverse fantasies.

Whether it be Sergeant Fottrell and bicycles, De Selby and his D.M.P., or Joyce among the Jesuits, each character and his obsession expose the folly of modern efforts to define time. Rather than clarifying matters, these theories, at the very least, further muddle our understanding of time, and, at the very worst, lead to distortions of reality. On one level, because they are so abstract or so remote from human experience, they are perceptible, as Rampion says, only through non-human eyes. On another level, however, they can lead to potentially harmful efforts to manipulate reality by those who take the theories as literal truths.

Though O'Brien exploits, for the sake of parody, the abstract nature of time theories by creating characters who take microphysical or macroscopic theories quite literally, he finally seems much more interested in the dangers of intellectual manipulation in *The Dalkey Archive*. His focal point for this concern is Mick Shaughnessy, who gets so caught up in De Selby's plot to destroy the world that he, too, becomes a manipulator of reality. He is the narrative link between the Sergeant, De Selby, and Joyce, but he actually manipulates each one of these characters in his plan to save the world. He enlists the Sergeant in his plot to steal De Selby's D.M.P., tries to help Joyce join the Jesuits, and seriously contemplates introducing De Selby and Joyce in the hope that they become literary collaborators who will "devote their considerable brains in consultation to some recondite, involuted and incomprehensible literary project, ending in publication of a book which would be commonly ignored and thus be no menace to universal sanity" *(DA* 129).

Mick's motives are admirable and his reasoning, which implies that we would be living in a safer, saner world if Einstein had been an artist rather than a scientist, seems sound, but his hold on reality slips badly as he becomes more and more involved with the idea of stopping De Selby. He comes to believe that his mission has been assigned to him by God and that his role in life has risen to the stature of priest. In other words, Mick, because he convinces himself that his actions are now directed by God, absolves himself of all personal responsibility for his thoughts and actions. In this respect, he, too, is something of a parody of Stephen Dedalus, that priest of the eternal imagination, who is willing to sacrifice all human contact, feeling, and responsibility for the sake of his artistic mission. Mick actually out-Stephens Dedalus, because he decides that after he is finished with De Selby and Joyce, he will take on the "regular ecclesiastical faculties" *(DA* 156).

While pursuing his priestly mission, Mick becomes alienated from his friends and loved ones because he has lost both common sense and compassion. When he is brought back to his senses by Mary, who represents security and continuity, he returns to the normal world. However, O'Brien's green world (slightly tainted by cuckoldry) of love, marriage, and birth is so ordinary compared to the mad and fantastic worlds of Sergeant Fottrell, De Selby, and Joyce that most readers have found the novel, particularly its ending, flat and disappointing, even though O'Brien believed that it was his best work. Yet O'Brien's offer of common sense and compassion as an antidote to intellectual manipulation supports Rampion's argument and ironically parallels the values inherent in the writings of James Joyce and St. Augustine, two characters drawn from history and parodied because of the preposterous images of each invented by humbug historians, theologians, and biographers. St. Augustine, after confessing his humanity, rejected any spatial concept of time and accepted only the human experiences of memory, attention, and expectation as conditions of temporality. Joyce, while pretending he was not human, relied upon the recurrent values and myths of the family for the themes and structures of *Ulysses* and *Finnegans Wake*.

At Swim-Two-Birds and *The Third Policeman* are not too different in conception from *The Dalkey Archive,* even though the techniques of the earlier novels are more elaborate and the humor more fantastic. Ironically, however, while the earlier novels are far more interesting for the critics, they are not as encompassing in their time themes as *The Dalkey Archive*. For all its mad dimensions, *At Swim-Two-Birds* is limited thematically to the world of art, particularly the tendency in some writers and readers to substitute literature for life, a grievous fault in literary critics (Joyceans are most susceptible) and literary-minded types like Walter Bidlake in *Point Counter Point*. Structurally, *The Third Policeman* parallels no less than Dante's *Inferno,* but it, too, is more limited than *The Dalkey Archive* because the dimensions of its hell are purely pseudoscientific.

Though O'Brien finished the manuscript of *The Third Policeman* by 1940, the book was not published until 1967, some three years after the publication of *The Dalkey Archive*. The failure to find a publisher for *The Third Policeman* for so many years eventually prompted O'Brien to use some of his material in his later novel, the most blatant example being Sergeant Fottrell's "Mollycule" theory, which appears as

Sergeant Pluck's atomic theory in *The Third Policeman*. De Selby is also used in both novels, but for entirely different reasons. In *The Dalkey Archive*, De Selby is an actual character, a pneumatic chemist, who has mastered time with his D.M.P. and hopes to destroy the world with it. His mad scheme is a major part of a pattern of speculation and manipulation that shapes the novel. In *The Third Policeman*, de Selby (whose name is spelled with a lower case *d*) appears only through his theories and the writings of his commentators. As a parody of the pseudoscientific mind, he is a comic counter point to the hell prepared for the narrator, who has robbed and murdered old Mathers for the money to publish a complete edition of de Selby's work and has been murdered, in turn, by Divney, his partner in the crime.

O'Brien's parody of the scientific theorist is clearly evident in the novel's mock-footnotes, which offer elaborate explanations of de Selby's ideas as well as the attacks and apologies made by de Selby's commentators. Among de Selby's theories, which in themselves are parodies of relativist and serial concepts of reality, are his conclusions that the earth, rather than being a sphere, is sausage-shaped; that night, rather than being the result of planetary movement, is caused by black air or the staining of the atmosphere by invisible volcanic eruptions; that a man standing in front of a mirror rather than seeing a true reflection, actually sees an image of himself as a younger man; and that time, rather than being duration, is nothing more than a succession of brief, static experiences. De Selby made this last discovery of the spatial reality of time after examining a reel of a cinematograph film—once again proving O'Brien's rule that a little bit of knowledge can be a dangerous thing.

After finishing *The Third Policeman*, O'Brien wrote to William Saroyan that he had just done a story about a murderer who is dead, but does not know "that all the queer ghastly things which have been happening to him are happening in a sort of hell which he earned for the killing."[8] O'Brien's vision of hell is clearly Dantesque. Not only is it circular, but it imposes on the nameless narrator (one of his punishments is that he cannot remember his name) a punishment made up of literal transcriptions of de Selby's theories. Since de Selby is a parody of time theorists like Einstein and Dunne and the interpreters of their theories, this de Selbyish hell is a riot of minute particles, light waves, serial observers, and time loops. Our narrator, after murdering a man for de Selby's theories, faces an eternity of a recurring world literally created out of the half-truths, distortions, and absurdities that make up the best of de Selby's work.

Of all the modern time theories that plague the narrator of *The Third Policeman,* those of J. W. Dunne seem the most compelling. His serialism defines the levels or circles of hell in O'Brien's *Inferno,* and his ideas on dreams and eternity clarify the identity of the third policeman. In Dunne's theory of serial time, as explained earlier, the measurement of duration is possible only if we accept the idea of an observer on a different time level, whose actions are viewed and judged by an observer on still another level, and so on. Dunne believed that these observers (he emphasized three) take on more and more dimensions until we arrive finally at an Absolute Observer. In *The Third Policeman,* Dunne's first observer is the narrator whose only level of understanding is the three-dimensional world of sensory and memory phenomena. His nightmarish hell, however, is four-dimensional, thereby bewildering his senses and leaving him with no clear identity. The second observer, who attends to and judges what the first observer does, is represented by the policemen, Pluck and MacCruiskeen. Pluck's atomic theory and MacCruiskeen's spear and elaborate chests illustrate their control over the four-dimensional world of modern physics. There is, however, another observer who controls and manipulates all the levels of hell and corresponds to Dunne's Absolute Observer. This God- or Satan-like observer is none other than Mr. Fox, the third policeman. Because he possesses omnium, which is the form of forms or the essence of the universe, he has the ultimate power to change reality by manipulating time and space:

> If I could believe him he had been sitting in this room presiding at four ounces of this inutterable substance,

calmly making ribbons of the natural order, inventing intricate and unheard of machinery to delude the other policemen, interfering drastically with time to make them think they had been leading their magical lives for years, bewildering, horrifying and enchanting the whole countryside. [*TP* 188]

Omnium is the common element linking the parody of science in *The Third Policeman* and that in *The Dalkey Archive,* where De Selby's D.M.P. is the substance capable of interfering with time and reality. The major difference between the novels is the fate of the two main characters: Mick Shaughnessy comes to his senses, whereas the narrator of *The Third Policeman* has no exit, and at the end of the novel, is about to repeat his nightmarish experiences. O'Brien, using the *persona* of Joe, the narrator's newly discovered soul, wrote that hell eternally "goes round and round. In shape it is circular and by nature it is interminable, repetitive and very nearly unbearable."[9] He could have added that hell is unbearable because its reality reflects our own distortions and misunderstandings of the truth.

As a symbol of the capacity of scientific theory to manipulate reality, omnium represents only one side of O'Brien's concern with notions that distort our perception of the true nature of things. In *At Swim-Two-Birds,* it is the artist's pen, rather than science, that plays havoc with reality. The equivalent of omnium in O'Brien's first novel is the theory of aestho-autogamy. As a literary phenomenon, it either eliminates conception and pregnancy or reduces "these processes to the same mysterious abstraction as that of the paternal factor in the commonplace case of unexplained maternity." In other words, aestho-autogamy gives the writer the power to create living characters *super spottum* or, like the holy spirit, to impregnate with the word a woman who will give birth some nine months later. What aestho-autogamy leads to in *At Swim-Two-Birds* is a series of outrageous literary events that completely subvert the normal order of time. We have characters being born instantly into adulthood and a writer so enamored with one of his female creations that he rapes her. We also have that same female character giving birth to the writer's son, who then seeks vengeance upon his father because his mother died in childbirth—an event not surprising considering her son was an adult at birth.

All this time and tomfoolery is part of O'Brien's parody of the notion shared by some artists and their most ardent critics, that art is life, or, even worse, that art, as a higher form of reality, has dominion over life. *At Swim-Two-Birds* has several levels of narration that give O'Brien free play in having fun with the idea that art is superior to life. On one level, the novel consists of several routine biographical reminiscences of a first-person narrator, a university student, who is writing a novel. The fun begins when the narrator creates a writer, Dermot Trellis, who is also writing a novel. The narrative becomes outrageous when characters created by Trellis (who steals material from William Tracy, a writer of Irish cowboy stories) become unhappy with their lot and collaborate on a novel chiefly written by Orlick Trellis, the son of Dermot, to revenge themselves upon their creator, who has been invented by the narrator of a book being written by Flann O'Brien.

The outcome of all this is a parody of several assumptions made about the art of fiction, particularly the books written by Joyce, and about the art of criticism, particularly Oscar Wilde's platonic dialogues, which portray the critic as the supreme artist. *At Swim-Two-Birds* mocks the novel as autobiography, epic, dream, and even revenge-book. It also pokes fun at the idea of the writer as the Artist-God who is his own father and his own son and at the belief in the power of the imagination to create a world unto itself. By the novel's end, poor Dermot Trellis, the epitome of the writer who lives entirely within the world of his imagination, has his powers entirely usurped by his characters. They put him through an ordeal and trial that rival those of Bloom and Joseph K. for sheer physical and mental humiliation. He is saved only by his servant, who puts an end to all this nonsense by accidentally burning several sheets of writing which had created Trellis's tormentors.

While all these preposterous literary events are taking place, practically every character in *At Swim-Two-Birds* steps forward to express himself as a literary critic. This leads to a variety of comments on plot and characterization, the novel as moral instruction, and art as an expression of the common folk. O'Brien also has some fun with the modern artist's tendency to plunder the literature of the past and with the critic's obsession with literary borrowings. The narrator offers an aesthetic based on the idea that the "entire corpus of existing literature should be regarded as a limbo from which discerning authors could draw their characters as required, creating only when they failed to find a suitable existing puppet. The modern novel should be largely a work of reference. Most authors spend their time saying what has been said before—usually said much better" *(STB* 33).

Two other aspects of the narrator's aesthetic clearly reveal what is behind O'Brien's literary games in *At Swim-Two-Birds.* The narrator also says that if modern writers add a "wealth of reference" to their works it would eliminate the critic's job of offering tiresome explanations of character, theme, and structure and would effectively preclude the pseudo-critics or what the narrator calls "mountebanks, upstarts, thimbleriggers and persons of inferior education" *(STB* 33) from ever understanding modern literature. The surviving readers would then have the opportunity to read novels that are obvious shams, that make no pretensions to being more real than life, and that allow the reader to "regulate at will the degree of his credulity" *(STB* 33).

While the aesthetic is obviously a parody of the relationship between Joyce and his host of explicators, it also justifies the delightful insanity of *At Swim-Two-Birds,* a novel that explains itself and never really pretends to be anything more than it is. For O'Brien, the novel should be a bash in the tunnel, a chance to have a good time at someone else's expense, while discovering and experiencing what the Pooka calls "the seam between night and day, that is an aesthetic delight." *At Swim-Two-Birds* proves O'Brien's point that literature should not be taken too seriously, that it should be read for its potential fun and joy. His second novel, *The Third Policeman*, reflects the same view about scientific theory as it parodies the distortions of reality perpetuated in the name of science. What emerges in O'Brien's later novels, first through the squalor of *The Hard Life* and finally through the combined parody of art and science in *The Dalkey Archive*, is a warning against manipulators of reality, while at the same time the manipulation itself is a justification for art. Madness, for O'Brien, becomes a dangerous malady when it expresses itself as a political act (the manipulation of people) or a scientific one (the manipulation of reality). The former can cause delusions about a master race and lead to the mass murder of millions of people, while the latter justifies tampering with nature even for the sake of discovering a doomsday weapon.

Madness, however, is a blessing when it creates art, because it gives us an occasional bash in the tunnel, a chance to slip through a crack in time and make the sorrows and fears of life more bearable when we return. As violent as O'Brien could become on the subject of James Joyce, he also said that Joyce's great gift was his humor. The implication of this statement and the themes of O'Brien's fiction are that the world can afford a few more jokes like *Ulysses* and *Finnegans Wake*, but not another plan for a master race or the invention of the ultimate bomb.

NOTES

1. This excerpt of a 17 December 1941 column is quoted in *A Flann O'Brien Reader*, ed. Stephen Jones (New York: Viking, 1978), p. 33.

2. Flann O'Brien, *At Swim-Two-Birds* (London: MacGibbon & Kee, 1966), p. 12. Subsequent references are indicated parenthetically in the text by *STB* and the page number(s).

3. Aldous Huxley, *Point Counter Point* (New York: Harper & Row, 1965), p. 406.

4. Ibid., p. 129.

5. Ibid.

6. Flann O'Brien, *The Dalkey Archive* (New York: Macmillan, 1964), p. 86. Subsequent references are indicated parenthetically in the text by *DA* and the page number(s).

7. This excerpt of a letter from O'Brien to Timothy O'Keefe of MacGibbon & Kee is quoted in *A Flann O'Brien Reader*, p. 374.

8. Flann O'Brien, *The Third Policeman* (New York: Walker & Co., 1967), p. 200. (The letter is quoted in the publisher's note on the last page of this edition.) Subsequent references are indicated parenthetically in the text by *TP* and the page number(s).

9. Published as part of the publisher's note attached to O'Brien, *The Third Policeman*, p. 200.

Waking the Dead: *The Islandman* and the Irish Revival
By John Wilson Foster

We have accounted for the bulk of Irish Revival fiction when we account for two kinds of writing, some of which we might call "para-fiction" or near-fiction: translations, redactions, and adaptations of, on the one hand, Irish heroic romances (chiefly from the Old and Middle Irish manuscripts), and of, on the other hand, folktales, field collected during the Revival or published (usually with grave literary distortion) before the Revival. Consideration of the mutual processes of translation, redaction, and adaptation, to which the saga and folktale were subjected, allows us to unify a diverse field. The career of the Irish saga during the Revival involves work as varied as that produced by Kuno Meyer and the scholarly translators; P. W. Joyce, Standish James O'Grady, Eleanor Hull, Lady Gregory, and other popularizers; and O'Grady, AE, James Stephens, and other fictionizers. Similarly, the folktale category would include work by Patrick Kennedy, Lady Gregory, W. B. Yeats, Douglas Hyde, William Larminie, and other collectors and anthologists; and by Stephens, Padraic Colum, Yeats, Lord Dunsany, and other fictionizers and fabricators. The search for fictional forms of saga and folktale is a Revival characteristic. So too is the penchant for past or preserved literatures, and the fact that this inclination was in geographic and psychic terms westward rather than eastward (even the bardic literature was made to seem a west Irish literature). We might add, too, that the *summum bonum*, the ideal to which literary form and content aspired, even where the heroic romance was concerned, was selflessness, which I believe ultimately lends the Irish Literary Revival its identity.

What Revival fiction writers have I not mentioned? Chiefly Joyce and Moore, of course, whose membership in the Revival must be highly qualified. We might recall that Sean O'Faolain thought in 1947 that only a dozen realistic Irish novels had been written, six of which (and four of those by Joyce and Moore) had been written between 1887 and 1926, the years roughly of the Revival.[1] It is possible that Joyce believed that in "The Dead" he was raising and laying to rest the ghost of Ireland past, a ghost that walked the primitive West and, if the Revivalists had anything to do with it, would come east and to life; that he was, in several senses, waking the dead. Perhaps he felt that as a modern fiction writer he would be hampered by the fashionable blandishments of the countryside, of the peasantry, of the West, of folklore, as well as of the aristocratic bardic literature and the heroic past it preserved. To the extent that he was a modern British and European novelist, he preferred to operate from a middle-class urban milieu and with a concern for ethical, rational, and individual man in society, an east in the compelling westwardness of the Revival, to adapt Wallace Stevens on Kerry. The nuance of personal circumstance cannot be overlooked. As an Irishman from a family whose fortunes were declining and an Irishman who had actually derived from the West in a profounder sense than had Protestant writers such as Yeats and Synge, Joyce rejected romantic primitivism, as did Catholic writers after him, such as Frank O'Connor, Patrick Kavanagh, and O'Faolain. Yet because of the West's still potent reality for him, Joyce was more painfully ambivalent towards it than were the Protestants. The West's awake, announced Thomas Davis, and to his chagrin Gabriel Conroy in "The Dead" finds that it is true, the ghost of Ireland's past coming the closer as Conroy himself nears sleep. Here, as in *A Portrait of the Artist as a Young Man*, the West imposes itself upon the governing consciousness of the narrative—hero's and author's—and demands homage, which it receives in the romantic figure of

Michael Furey. At story's end, however, Joyce, having entertained the West against his will, as it were, intentionally buries it, with all else, under the snow that falls on Oughterard cemetery, on the mutinous Shannon waves and all through the universe. There was to be no easy or decisive victory for the romantic primitivism of the Revival.

As this last phrase implies, it was no realistic West Joyce was burying, though the fact that Michael Furey worked in the gasworks is a Joycean stroke of ironic realism. Little more was there a realistic West in the fiction of the most ardent champions of the peasantry who in life travelled there. The writers I mentioned in connection with folktales were largely writing *about* the peasantry, even on occasions tampering with collected folklore in accordance with a desired literary and social image of the peasant. Until after the Revival (and in a sense despite the Revival), perhaps Carleton is as close as we get to a peasant author committing himself, his upbringing, ambitions and inner feelings, to paper. And Carleton, an Ulsterman, thought of himself as of the Irish yeomanry, not peasantry! The peasant had scant access to sophisticated means of self-expression, so others put words in his mouth and ideas in his head. Lover's comic peasant, Pearse's Christian peasant, Yeats's mystic peasant, Joyce's half-contemptible, half-mysterious peasant (the old man Mulrennan met, for example, at the end of *A Portrait*): all of these we have and more. But where during the Revival are the autobiographies and fictions written by the remote countryman himself?

The answer is that it was not until the Revival virtually ended as a self-contained literary movement of undoubted excellence that such works, because of and in ironic contradiction to the Revival, appeared. A "striking triptych"[2] of Gaelic peasant autobiographies, for example, were written in the nineteen twenties and thirties by three Blasket islanders, Tomás Ó Crohan, Peig Sayers, and Maurice O'Sullivan. Here was a new Irish literary genre, of which there have been at least six later examples, though the genre is obviously incapable of longevity. All three Blasket autobiographies are in part elegies and obituaries as well as celebrations and thefts from time. The soulful remark at the close of the first and best, Ó Crohan's *The Islandman,* became famous enough to be parodied by Flann O'Brien in *The Poor Mouth (An Béal Bocht):* "I have done my best to set down the character of the people about me so that some record of us might live after us, for the like of us will never be again."[3] It was prophetic: the Blaskets were abandoned in 1953. *An t-Oileánach* was written in the early 1920s and published in 1929, and apparently came as a blinding revelation to Gaelic-speaking readers and scholars. Here were "the real facts of Irish life, of the Hidden Ireland we might say, in the mother tongue for the very first time," said one scholar.[4] No less of a revelation must it have been to English-speaking readers when it appeared as *The Islandman* in 1934, translated by Robin Flower. Written at the tail end of the Revival, translated well after it, *The Islandman* itself commemorates three "ages" as Ó Crohan sees them: the "savage age" before the 1850s (known to Ó Crohan through hearsay and legend), the "heroic age" of Ó Crohan's childhood and youth (roughly 1856–75), and the "age of decline" (roughly and ironically the decades of the Revival). (The historical shadow and spread of the book, from Blasket legendary to Ireland in 1934, is therefore vast.) Of the first age Ó Crohan speaks with awe, of the second with laconic fondness and nostalgia, of the third with stoic gloom. In both Irish and English versions, *The Islandman* is one of the ornaments of twentieth-century Irish literature. It is the utterance of a singular and ancient voice speaking to us in understandably muffled tones across intervening centuries that have not in fact passed at all. Yet if we listen carefully, the voice sounds ambiguous. It is not just that of archaic man but, less assured, of modern Irish man awakening, in a remote and isolated pocket of existence, from archaism into selfhood. Twentieth-century Ireland, herself in the period costume of the literary movement, disturbs the sleep of the island; time disturbs timelessness, place placelessness, fact legend. And that is not all.

The Islandman, claims Sean O'Tuama, "is more the

biography of an island community than of a single islander,"[5] and on a first reading we are likely to agree, as we accompany the islanders in their communal though often competitive pursuits, their rugged commensalism. But they cannot be taken without qualification to represent The West. Despite the frequent and sometimes heroically maiming factionalism (for the hand if lifted readily and even fellow-islanders can be callously cast adrift on the open sea), the Blasketmen knew themselves to be different from outsiders, to be "certain set apart," to use Yeats's phrase. "We had characters of our own," writes Ó Crohan, "each different from the other, and all different from the landsmen . . . we are not to be put in comparison with the people of the great cities or of the soft and level lands" *(Islandman* 321–22). Inexorably, however, centralized authority with (in times of island defiance) its superior firepower and, after Home Rule, a new altruistic, even more damaging mandate, exerts an intrusive power and influence. So does the outside world, at first merely Dunquin, Ventry, dimly Tralee, rarely Valencia, and at the end, Dublin, England, Scandinavia, and the eastern world, in comparison to which the island shrinks and discovers itself.

The Islandman is the authentic inside information, social observation, and documentary realism Revival writers would have required to write a genuine rural fiction of the West, but did not possess, bar possibly Synge who was of the opinion that "To write a real novel of the island life one would require to pass several years among the people. . . . "[6] Nor could they have come into its possession without, as Synge did, disrupting in however slight a degree the fragile equilibrium of island life. But I think O'Tuama's is only half the story and even then one that does not wholly accord with Revival concepts of the islanders and the West generally, as I have just implied. By subtler signals than Ó Crohan's personal hardship and tragedy have we the impression of a man apart from his fellows. In the early chapters we meet a boy who will become special, himself "certain set apart," not because he can bring ill-luck with a satiric verse like the island poet Dunlevy, but because he is a sharp-tongued and sharp-witted observer.

(And unlike the poet Dunlevy he is an island Renaissance man of Crusoe-like versatility—fine dancer, hunter, fisherman, singer, house-builder, poet, turf-cutter, storyteller.) There is a circumspection, a sternness in him, a moralistic detachment most evident when he is islanded in vigilant sobriety during the Blasketman's epic drinking bouts. He is almost, it seems, the self-appointed conscience of the island, a primitive forerunner (actually elder contemporary) of Joyce. On occasions he even uses this unique opportunity to pay off old scores against those who failed to reach his exacting standards of loyalty, as Joyce sometimes used his fiction. In *The Islandman*, then, is an emerging integrity and individuality of hero and voice that go against the grain of Revival philosophy and are expressively autobiographical in tenor.

A duality analogous to Ó Crohan's status as an islander is exhibited by the form and style of *The Islandman*. It has a pronounced oral accent, and avoids, Flower tells us, the literary "cramp-Irish" *(Islandman* xii). It is also strewn with scraps of folklore. Ó Crohan delivers himself of numerous proverbs whose dexterous use in Irish-speaking communities is a sign of learning and eloquence. He can several times toss off a quotation from the Finn sagas (oars are "tough, sweet-sounding, enduring, white, broad bladed") and in his "Foreword" Flower assures us of Ó Crohan's prowess as a tale-teller. We are treated to a hint of Ó Crohan's ability with the traditional long tale in his account of his combat with a beached seal which, as O'Tuama rightly says, takes on "the proportions of an epic act of Achilles." J. V. Luce, the Greek scholar, has in fact tried to show analogies between life and literature on Great Blasket and the Homeric epics and the early Ionian way of life.[7]

Yet the combat also exhibits the initiative of Crusoe and the particularity of Defoe. Indeed, in *The Islandman* as a whole, Ó Crohan, working out of a primitive mentality and archaic sense of time, wrests history and objectivity. It is a birth and a forgetting; only twelve out of twenty-five chapters can be precisely dated. Ó Crohan's sense of history is chiefly provided by the customs that died during his lifetime, the eating of seal meat, sobriety at wakes, and so on; and by positive innovations: the first tea (found as salvage and thought to be a dye), the first spectacles (thought to be worn by a man from hell by the schoolchildren), and the first steamship (thought to be a sailing ship on fire by the islanders who rowed fruitlessly after it).

As well as enhancing chronology and fact by putting in abeyance a traditional understanding, Ó Crohan was constrained by his advisor to tell a life-*story*, and we can read his somewhat painful efforts through primitive chapter linkage to cast his life into a narrative. But the pull of the book is toward independent tales, be they the ghosts of voyage or wonder tales, *Echtrai* or *Märchen*. His anecdotes about sharks and "sea-beasts" resemble the sea-monster legends collected by Lady Gregory in *Visions and Beliefs in the West of Ireland*. On such occasions we see fact and rudimentary (or vestigial) legend mingle. Since the facts concern Ó Crohan's life and since the suggestion of folk-anecdote in his telling of them remains, we might describe *The Islandman* as an extended memorat, a form of personal tradition, the recording of which Lady Gregory helped to pioneer by encouraging her informants to talk about themselves, as a Mr. O'Kelly did Ó Crohan. In such a tradition, the content of personal experience tends to be poured into the mould of folk-expression. To be one's own hero through an extended narrative is not congenial to the traditional storyteller and Ó Crohan takes understandable refuge in anecdote, and when he feels he must comment on himself does so with an engagingly self-deprecating humor. There is, however, a sufficiently shaped and sustained awareness of self for us to call *The Islandman* a genuine autobiography, newly emerged from mere folk information and the memorat. Flower also refers to the distinctive personality of Ó Crohan's prose style. The book is a further transition, then, in the gradual emergence from obscurity of the Irish folk teller or informant and, by that token, the Irish peasant. Subordinate in the 19th century to the collectors and then his cicerones and notaries, he at last becomes a writer whose fame exceeds that of his mentors.

But there is some silent irony in the fact that although it salvages folkways and folklore from the smother of the past,

The Islandman itself, in conception and effect (it was conceived as literature, not oral testimony), was part of what helped to kill the traditional oral lore of the Blasket Islands. Ó Crohan recalls procuring his first books during the Irish Revival and how when he read the collected stories to the islanders they lost the taste for telling those same stories in their own ways. The men who encouraged Ó Crohan to read were those who bemoaned the loss of the folktale because of the incursive tyranny of print. The irony seems to have escaped Synge, for example, when in *The Aran Islands* he tells us that in his cottage a young islander is reading Douglas Hyde's *Beside the Fire* (presumably Synge's own copy) and then that such books are discouraging young people from learning stories from their elders. Synge also fails to see the irony in his generous gift of a clock to Aran Islanders who had no clock and worked by hunger and shadow: "when I tell them what o'clock it is by my watch they are not satisfied, and ask how long is left them before the twilight."[8] Now, thanks to Synge, they became acquainted with the petty tyranny of chronometric time.

The western islands were undergoing damaging changes in their traditional way of life in any case during the years of the Revival. The introduction of modern implements, customs, and points of view accelerated; internal problems caused by peculiar inheritance and marriage systems, and such acts of God as alterations in the migration habits of fish shoals, grew more acute. Flower recalls major changes in the agricultural and social pattern of settlement Great Blasket underwent between 1910 and 1930, changes more numerous in his opinion than in all the previous years of the island's existence. Meanwhile there were the tax men, the First World War, foreign fishing fleets, and the Home Rule crisis, all impinging on island life.[9] Synge for his part noted significant changes in the life of the Aran Islands before and after 1898: the emergence of class, rank and division of labor; the advent of prosperity; the appearance of the criminal mind (which Synge blames on the introduction of police); the decline of Gaelic.

These changes the scholars and enthusiasts of the Revival quickened. They waked the dead in an opposite fashion to

Joyce: they aroused and celebrated the West on purpose but helped to bury it unintentionally. The continuation of those features for which the West was lauded, variously described as primitive, archaic, prehistoric, medieval, and pagan, depended precisely upon western life remaining incompatible with grandiose Revivalist notions espoused in that native colonialism that was the cultural renaissance. The Revivalists could not have their unreformed West (a West frequently uninterested in nationalism and the Irish language, as Synge found to be the case on the Aran Islands) and their revival too. The western islands attracted the Revivalists chiefly because of an isolation that was in fact more complete under the neglect of English rule than under the solicitude of Home Rule fervor. "I often told the fishermen," Ó Crohan remembered, "that Home Rule had come to the Irish without their knowing it, and that the first beginning of it had been made in the Blasket now that the yellow gold of England and France was coming to our thresholds to purchase our fish, and we didn't give a curse for anybody" *(Islandman* 206–07). It would be difficult to imagine a notion of independence more removed from the mystical nationalism of Pearse. I suspect that some of the Revivalists were unhappy with this kind of attitude and wanted to change, not preserve, contemporary island life in accordance with their picture of the noble past of the island, one very different from Ó Crohan's "savage age." I suspect too that other Revivalists realized that revival, even preservation, was impossible. Revival midwives such as Flower were, it might be thought, engaged in inducing a cultural rebirth on the islands, but the feverishness of their activities suggests that they sensed that island life and lore were doomed and felt that they should be recorded, even if in the process the doom was hastened. There was a birth, certainly, we have evidence and no doubt, but it was like death and it was those who were visited, such as Ó Crohan, not the journeyers, who were no longer at ease in the old dispensation. In a double irony, the Revival helped give articulate tongue to a self-consciousness that was incompatible with Revival ideals (as Joyce's fiction proves on another scale); but as for the archaic western island, as it expressed itself, it succumbed, like some lowly species of animal for whom death and reproduction are one and the same.

According to Flower, "it would probably never have occurred to Tomás to write his life, had it not been for Mr. Brian O'Kelly of Killarney, who encouraged him to set about the work, and read over part of Maxim Gorki's autobiography to him to show the interest of that kind of writing" *(Islandman* xiv). As a matter of fact, there is little resemblance between *The Islandman* and Gorki's *Childhood.* Nor is there much resemblance between Ó Crohan's work and Pierre Loti's novel, *An Iceland Fisherman,* a romantic insight into the folkways of Breton fishermen, which O'Kelly also read to Ó Crohan: perhaps O'Kelly's choice of this book was occasioned by Synge's fondness for it, and his choice of Gorki occasioned by Patrick Pearse's advocacy of the Russian to Gaelic fiction writers as an antidote to Dickens and to the folktale. Be that as it may, literary affinities are probably more illuminating than literary stimuli; O'Tuama provocatively suggests the autobiographies of American Indians that describe their ancestral life before the triumph of the white man. *Black Elk Speaks* might be a useful starting-point for comparison. Certainly the Indian testimonies have in common with the Blasket autobiographies the record of a doomed society. Be this too as it may, the fact remains that Ó Crohan was exposed to highly crafted and self-consciously literary works before writing *The Islandman.*

If *The Islandman* can be regarded as proto-history and proto-geography, it can also be regarded as proto-novel, having its beginnings in letters (to O'Kelly) as though in imitation of some 18th century early novels. There are some blatantly fictional techniques, for example the re-creation of scenes, complete with dialogue, at which Ó Crohan was not in fact present, and Ó Crohan's ironic self-image which is one created not just by a humble man but one with an eye on persona and effect. The fictional possibilities of autobiography were, of course, seen more clearly by Maurice O'Sullivan, a much younger contemporary whose *Twenty Years A-Growing* nevertheless appeared only four years after *The Islandman.* (The famous dream sequence in O'Sullivan was in fact a Blasket tale fictionally and silently appropriated.) Other writers, not always islanders, were quick to see the fictional value of the western island as a social and political microcosm. The documentary resemblance between *The Islandman* and *Islanders* (1927) by Peadar O'Donnell, a Donegal man, is the more remarkable because, as far as I know, O'Donnell wrote his novel of life on a Donegal island without knowledge of Ó Crohan's finished but not yet published work. This being so, we cannot say on evidence of direct comparison that *Islanders*, a much more plotted work than Ó Crohan's, is an example of the raising of "low" forms that formalists have identified as a method of literary regeneration,[10] but it seems to me that this kind of regeneration characterizes the Irish Literary Revival, particularly its fiction, that *The Islandman* is a startling example of what we might call self-raising literary form, and that Ó Crohan's work enacts the early development of the novel almost two centuries after it had occurred. The special Revivalist genre to which *The Islandman* belongs, then, is threefold—it is folklore, history (including autobiography), and fiction.

Because they were already established in rural Irish fiction since Carleton, the themes of rural decline and individual dissatisfaction with life on the land are foreground in *Islanders* where they are only potential foreground in *The Islandman*. To become dissatisfied with island shortcomings, as Ó Crohan dimly begins to do, is to become aware of the island as island. In the old tales the western Irish are orientated toward the sea, and it is in the infinite West that the imaginary islands were to be found. *The Islandman* is still a portion of that mythology but it also charts an inclination toward the east, away from the sea. Between these two orientations Tomás Ó Crohan stands Janus-faced. Out of the dilemma emerges the self (like the dead awakening) which the island comes to symbolize: a self suddenly vulnerable, unmoored from familiar and age-old beliefs, launched on a lonely search to understand and weigh the exotic values of the world. But it was not as the Revival thought; this sense of self could only be achieved at the expense of the island as Revival artifact. Gabriel Conroy and Joyce himself were similarly caught between two counterpart but more sophisticated orientations. It is as if Ó Crohan as a writer begins the long trek that ends for our purposes with Joyce, the Catholic, middle-class Dublin author of "The Dead," or as if Ó Crohan as hero begins the long trek that ends for our purposes with the Catholic middle-class Dubliner Gabriel Conroy, haunted by echoes of his dim origins in the West. To these extents *The Islandman* is a literary coelacanth, a contemporary forerunner, the bizarre re-run of the first reel of a marathon film. That the realization of self is as brief in *The Islandman* (considering the imminent extinction of the islanders) as Gabriel's in "The Dead" (before the self-transcending epiphany) is irrelevant; the trek itself and the symbolic accession are all. Besides, in so far as *The Islandman* encouraged Sayers and O'Sullivan to record almost for the first time the feelings of Irish western peasants, Ó Crohan was a pioneer, an unqualified precursor.

NOTES

1. Sean O'Faolain, *The Irish: A Character Study* (Harmondsworth: Penguin Books, 1969), p. 130.
2. The phrase is Riobárd P. Breatnach's in his "Foreword" to his translation of Conchúr Ó Siocháin's *Seanchas Chléire, The Man From Cape Clear* (Dublin: The Mercier Press, 1975), p. ix.
3. Tomás Ó Crohan, *The Islandman*, trans. Robin Flower (London: Chatto and Windus, 1934), p. 323. Subsequent references to the book and to Flower's "Foreword" (pp. vii–xiv) will be indicated parenthetically in the text by "*Islandman*" and the page number(s).
4. Breatnach, "Foreword" to Conchúr Ó Siocháin's *Seanchas Chléire, The Man From Cape Clear*, p. viii.
5. Sean O'Tuama, "The other Tradition: Some Highlights of Modern Fiction in Irish," in *The Irish Novel in Our Time*, ed. Patrick Rafroidi and Maurice Harmon (Lille: Publications de l'Université de Lille III, 1975–76), p. 39.
6. A notebook entry quoted in J. M. Synge, *Collected Works*, Vol. II: *Prose*, ed. Alan Price (London: Oxford University Press, 1966), p. 102n.
7. J. V. Luce, "Homeric Qualities in the Life and Literature of the Great Blasket Island," *Greece & Rome*, n. s. 16(October 1969): 151–68.
8. *Collected Works: Prose*, p. 66.
9. Robin Flower, *The Western Island or The Great Blasket* (Oxford: The Clarendon Press, 1944).
10. Robert Scholes, *Structuralism in Literature: An Introduction* (New Haven and London: Yale University Press, 1974), p. 176.

Austin Clarke: The Poet's Image of Frustrated Love
By Beth S. Timson

Austin Clarke thought of love as a force flowing strongly in its own natural channels, but, when damned or diverted, turning swiftly into a force potentially vengeful and destructive. Though his writing spanned fifty years, moving from the patriotic fervor of the Easter Rising of 1916 to the world-weary satire of the sixties, still Clarke remained remarkably constant to one central image: the image of the tormented and frustrated lover. He casts this image into two *personae* who recur again and again in all the periods of his work and in every mode from epic to lyric to satiric.

The first of these two figures is the woman; whatever her name, she is free and sensual, sacrificing everything for love, only to be used and then rejected by a masculine world. The second figure is that of the prophet-scholar; he burns with a love for his homeland which scorns his words whether of praise or censure. It is the image of Parnell, the image perhaps of Yeats and Joyce. Together these two *personae* are ultimately the image of the poet himself.

When Clarke began his writing career, the single theme that seemed to be going to dominate his work was not love but Irish nationalism and the Celtic Twilight madness. In his case it was perhaps inescapable. He studied at the National University under Gaelic scholars Douglas Hyde, George Sigerson, and Stephen MacKenna, and his mentor was poet and rebel Thomas MacDonagh; he took deeply to heart MacDonagh's final words before his execution: "We do not claim to represent the people of Ireland; we claim to represent the intellect and the immortal soul of Ireland."[1] His first works, thus, were epic narratives based almost entirely on the traditional Celtic legends—*The Vengeance of Fionn* in 1917, *The Sword of the West* in 1921, and *The Cattledrive in Connaught* in 1925. As Clarke later explained his own thinking, "My own early poems were of an epic kind for I had been influenced by Ferguson and Herbert Trench, and it seemed to me that only in a remote way could the primitive forces still in civilisation be expressed."[2]

The best of these early works, *The Vengeance of Fionn*, is taken fairly literally from the ancient tale *The Pursuit of Diarmuid and Grainne* and is heavily influenced by Trench's 1901 play *Déirdre Wedded.* Yet even in this work one can see the first stirrings of what was to become Clarke's governing personal myth of frustrated love. In the compelling madness of their passion, Diarmuid and Grainne flee from the jealous wrath of Fionn, but tragedy follows them closely:

> . . . Grainne, the wild, the beautiful, fled
> Up slopes of thickly clustered fern . . .
> ....
> . . . The wind ran with her
> And a voice cried: "O stay with us, O stay
> Lest thou should'st know of grief." But she
> Hastened up the mountain moor . . .[3]

When Diarmuid is at last drawn away from her, longing, as he says, "For the loud swords and the stern comrades" *(VF* 8), it is only Grainne who comes to a full recognition of the agony of lost love:

> "O Diarmuid, bitter it is
> Through the long nights, lying awake, alone,
> Stretching my arms to you in vain, in vain."
>
> *[VF* 18]

Loss and sorrow are also the threads in the other works of Clarke's early period. When he tried his hand at a religious poem, an imitation of the much-admired *Paradise Lost*, Clarke settled on the story of Moses; and the central image of that poem, *The Fires of Baal* (1921), is, in his own words, "the lonely death of Moses on Mount Nebo after his vision of the Promised Land."[4] Finally, from *The Sword of the West*, a series of poems on Cuchulain, we get the shorter work "The Sick-Bed of Cuchulain" in which the legendary hero, now aged and ailing, laments:

> "The wise men have seen the fires
> Going down and have gone to bed. I am
> Tired but they have left an aching in my joints
> That will not let me rest."[5]

Later in 1925, tired of being maligned by critics who would not see the essential modernity of his work, labelling him only a belated lingerer in the Celtic Twilight, Clarke bade his own farewell to Irish mythology in "Six Sentences," in lines reminiscent of Yeats's "The Coat" or Synge's "adieu" to "sweet Angus, Maeve, and Fand":

> The thousand tales of Ireland sink: I leave
> Unfinished what I had begun nor count
> As gain the youthful frenzy of those years.
> [CP 57]

He turned next to the medieval years, bringing with him his image of the sorrowful and frustrated lover, but hoping to find his audience most receptive to the common Western traditions of wandering clerks and cloistered monks than it had been to Cuchulain and Fionn. Too, this shift allowed him to focus attention on what he was coming more and more to stigmatize as the source of Ireland's psychic troubles: the Catholic Church.

Two poems in his medieval period, from the book *Pilgrimage and Other Poems* published in 1929, are the keys to his work in this mode. As he explained himself in a later critical work, his medieval poems were not vehicles of escape from problems, nor a refuge from present reality; instead, he felt that poetry, being "traditional and essentially romantic," had a better chance of reaching audiences if it "did not seek to chastise, but could use . . . the more subtle methods of sorrowful irony."[6] The first of these two poems of sorrowful irony is one of the Clarke poems regularly anthologized: "Aisling."

Aislings, which are Vision poems, were developed as a new style in the eighteenth century, primarily by Egan O'Rahilly who used them to symbolize the Jacobite hopes in Ireland; the poems usually feature the poet seeing a vision of beautiful woman, who is Ireland, mourning for her missing lover, either the Old or the Young Pretender. The popularity of aisling poems faded with Jacobite hopes.[7] Clarke chose to revive the old style in *Pilgrimage* because he felt that its blending of allegory and allusion suited his needs better than, as he says, "the inordinate claims of nineteenth century symbolism."[8]

In Clarke's "Aisling" the poet also encounters the woman who is Ireland, but in his version she is Ireland in her personification of Brigit—the pagan Celtic goddess who was claimed and canonized by the Catholic Church. To the unhappy poet's anguished questioning of her in the last stanza—

> "Shall I, too, find at dark of rain," I cried,
> "Neighbours around a fire cast up by the ocean
> And in that shining mansion hear the rise
> Of companies, or bide among my own—
> Pleasing a noble ear? O must I wander
> Without praise, without wine, in rich strange lands?"[9]

—she gives no answer but a smile.

The longest and perhaps the best poem in this middle period is Clarke's "The Young Woman of Beare," a response to a famous tenth-century poem "The Old Woman of Beare." The original poem is long and repetitious; its tone is easily seen in these three verses as translated by Frank O'Connor:

Austin Clarke: The Poet's Image of Frustrated Love 63

> For my hands as you may see
> Are but bony wasted things,
> Hands that once would grasp the hand,
> Clasp the haughty neck of kings.
> . . . .
> Welladay!
> Every child outlives its play,
> Year on year has worn my flesh
> Since my fresh sweet strength went grey.
> . . . .
> Floodtide!
> Flood or ebb upon the strand?
> What floodtide brings to you,
> Ebbtide carries from your hand.[10]
> . . . .

This poem, with its *memento mori* and *ubi sunt* motifs, was obviously intended as a warning to young women to avoid lives of sin, but Clarke has unerringly picked up the note of hypocrisy that sounds in the earlier poem and exposed it in "The Young Woman of Beare." That note in the pious message is that sin is really delightful fun and only growing old and unable to enjoy fleshly pleasures makes one philosophical about them. Clarke's young woman does not play the hypocrite in this matter as does her older counterpart. She openly revels in her sexuality: "I laze in yellow lamplight—/ . . . And laugh among lace pillows" *(LP* 15); and when she begins to have doubts about her soul they are honest ones, for oblivion in pleasure is still always within her grasp.

The change in the woman's mood from arrogant flaunting of sexuality to serious consideration of sin is brilliantly taken up and echoed in the language of the poem. The speaker, the woman, begins by associating herself with images of light and the Church with images of darkness: "praying people" hurry "Through lane or black archway" *(LP* 14), honest husbands only dream "at midnight" *(LP15* 15), and "black friars" preach of sin *(LP* 19); she is, however, "the bright temptation" *(LP* 14) who lies in "yellow lamplight" *(LP* 15), and she bares her "white haunch" of its "last bright stitch" for love *(LP* 16). But gradually she changes her imagery: she and her lover lie "Together in the dark" *(LP* 16), and she begins to call herself "the dark temptation" *(LP* 20), while the clergy become "shining orders" and prelates are "coped / With gold" *(LP* 20). The poem ultimately makes no judgments of morality, but its tightrope balance between sexual pleasure and sexual guilt, between the flesh and the soul, continues the question of whether, in Catholic Ireland, lovers of any kind can ever find happiness.

The medieval period provided the source of several of Clarke's most successful poems, and he returned to it occasionally in works after *Pilgrimage*—in isolated poems and in the prose romances *The Bright Temptation* (1932) and *The Singing Men at Cashel* (1936). The *Pilgrimage* volume contains also some of his best experiments in using internal assonance in place of rhyme and shows off his fine craftsmanship with words; the individual poem "Pilgrimage," for instance, contains the description of a monastery which is "a barren isle, / Where Paradise is praised" *(LP* 5), and on whose chapel windows "in stained glass the holy day / Was sainted" *(LP* 4).

But just as he had finally given up the mythological past for the middle ages, so Clarke was to give up the middle ages for the modern world. He had brought forward intact his image of frustrated love from the early epic verse into the lyrics on the medieval period, but its impact was still not strong enough on his audience. He felt a need and a pressure to write poems more openly critical of the Church and its stifling effect on Ireland. Accordingly, his volumes after the 1930s— *Night and Morning* in 1938, *Ancient Lights* in 1955, *Too Great a Vine* in 1957, *The Horse Eaters* in 1960, and *Flight to Africa and Other Poems* in 1963—deal directly and scathingly with social issues. His wit is sharp and precise, but never petty. As Thomas Kinsella observes, in these later poems "Small clear evils magnify into Evil, / Pity and mockery reflect a humane Good"; and Denis Donoghue echoes much the same sentiment: "there is a strange and wonderful synecdoche in these late poems, so that little things implicate big things, the Irish part stands for the human All."[11]

Speaking in a late prose work, the autobiographical *Twice Round the Black Church*, Clarke reports on what led him to open distrust of the Church, both wryly—"The Jesuit Fathers accepted the Victorian belief that the problems of puberty could be solved by the playing of British games, such as cricket or rugby," and more seriously—"There is no doubt that a country in which an ever-increasing number of celibate orders continually exert influence must suffer from a hidden uneasiness."[12] Thus the poet-scholar who speaks in "The Straying Student," the first poem in *Night and Morning*, has the right to be afraid of

> . . . this land, where every woman's son
> Must carry his own coffin and believe,
> In dread, all that the clergy teach the young.
> *[LP 37]*

Throughout these later poems, sharp images of sexuality and love, scorned, thwarted, and even brutally used by the Church, come into agonized focus. In *Ancient Lights*, in the poem "Marriage," he comments bitterly that "Parents are sinful now"; they

> . . . try to be chaste
> And when they cannot help it, steal the crumbs
> From their own wedding breakfast . . .
> . . . .
> But shall the sweet promise of the sacrament
> Gladden the heart, if mortals calculate
> Their pleasures by the calendar . . .
> . . . grow pale
> With guilty hope at every change of moon!
> *[LP 44]*

In *Flight to Africa*, the poem title "Living on Sin" only gains its full irony from the poem's content:

> The hasty sin of the young after a dance,
> Awkward in clothes against a wall or crick-necked
> In car, gives many a nun her tidy bed,
> Full board and launderette . . . [13]

As critic John Rees Moore comments most tellingly about Clarke, "His intellectuality and sensuality equally bring him into self-imposed debate with the tenets of Catholicism, from which, nevertheless, his values and even the categories of his emotional response are derived."[14]

The two key *personae* of these later volumes who develop the image first suggested with Grainne and Cuchulain back in the early epical works are the mad Maurice Devane in *Mnemosyne Lay in Dust* (1966) and "Martha Blake" in *Night and Morning* and "Martha Blake at Fifty-One" in *Flight to Africa*. Maurice spends his time in a Dublin insane asylum, trying desperately to remember something he has forgotten; he is the poet-scholar who has finally been driven into insanity by despair. In *Twice Round the Black Church* Clarke describes a fever-induced vision that inspired Maurice's fate: "I rushed, in dreams, through . . . institutions, full of miserable and thwarted souls, all of us in a frenzy trying to escape, yet imprisoned . . . —ingenuity bolted and barred by itself."[15] Maurice is not made sane until he is turned into a totally different person.

Mnemosyne Lay in Dust is a set of eighteen short poems, while the Martha Blake poems are two companion verses written years apart. If Martha Blake is fifty-one in 1963, the date of *Flight to Africa*, then one may assume she is a woman of twenty-six when Clarke first writes of her. She is a woman very reminiscent of Joyce's Eveline in *Dubliners*, trapped in a religion and culture so mind-suppressing that she is not even aware that she is trapped. The sensuality that was open in Grainne and at least enjoyed by the Young Woman of Beare has been in Martha Blake already controlled and broken to the service of the Church. She hurries to Mass in the mornings to kneel on "well-taught knees" (*LP* 32) and take communion with a tremble of emotions: "the priest is murmuring/ What she can scarcely tell" since "her heart/ Is making such a stir" *(LP* 32). Communion for her is a climactic experience; having eaten the wafer "now she feels within her breast/ Such calm that she is silent" *(LP* 33). The only unreal thing in her world is life itself, for Martha Blake is an addict of religion: "to begin the common day/ She needs a miracle" *(LP* 33).

In Clarke's usual careful way the words of the poem and their sounds reinforce the ironic meanings. The first stanza, for example, both echoes the bells ringing for Mass and subtly mocks Martha's one limited expression of sensuality:

> . . . the double bells are thrown back
> For Mass and echoes bound
> In the chapel yard, O then her soul
> Makes bold in the arms of sound.
> *[LP* 32]

Likewise, the priest's consecration of the Host is given the impact of an emotion-laden primitive ritual:

> She waits that dreaded coming,
> When all the congregation bows
> And none may look up.
> *[LP* 32]

And critic Christopher Ricks points out that Clarke in this poem deliberately violates his own assonance pattern in the sixth stanza to insert an anagram: Martha's soul is "silent" because her body is not permitted to "listen."[16]

"Martha Blake at Fifty-One" is a picture of what this particular young woman becomes. The body that she was trained to deny at twenty-six and the soul she was encouraged to nurture have grown even farther apart. Yet, while her thoughts are still all of saints and glory, the implicit sexual element in her religious faith has grown even stronger and more demanding for having been scorned. The saints that her thoughts rest longest upon are Teresa and John of the Cross;

dreaming of St. Teresa's visitation by the archangel, Martha swoons sympathetically "With pain and bliss as a dart / Moved up and down within her bowels" *(FA* 39–40), and meditating on St. John of the Cross she feels her spirit "In that divinest clasp, / . . . Yield to the soul-spasm" *(FA* 40).

Eventually, however, she is made to pay for her years of despising her body. As "To her pure thought, / Body was a distress" *(FA* 37) and had been ever since she had sublimated it to religion, so her body had come to hate her spirit: "Ill-natured flesh / Despised her soul" *FA* 40). The part of her self that she had scorned takes a brutal revenge upon her, driving her into a hospital where no one will believe that she is really ill:

> Mother Superior believed
>   That she was obstinate, self-willed.
> Sisters ignored her. . . .
> . . . .
>   They gave her purgatives.
> Soul-less, she tottered to the toilet.
>   Only her body lived.
>
> *[FA* 42]

Unreconciled to her self or her religion, she dies alone:

> . . . No priest
> Came. She had been anointed
> Two days before, yet knew no peace:
> Her last breath: disappointed.
>
> *[FA* 43]

The two Martha Blake poems are really Austin Clarke at his finest; the mockery is present but subdued beside the intensely human suffering of the woman whose whole life has been frustration. The emotional turmoil of thwarted love which Clarke openly described in *The Vengeance of Fionn* and gave epic proportions, which he portrayed as a subtle contest between action and guilt in "The Young Woman of Beare," has in the Martha Blake poems become concentrated into a burning focus on one tortured and agonizingly captured life.

It is a debatable point finally as to whether his image of thwarted love is better in his later or his earlier poems. He perhaps attempted more in his early poems and tried to express his convictions on the power of love in broader and more sweeping strokes, but one could argue that his talents show themselves to better advantage in the short satiric or lyric poem that emphasizes the quick image and the clean, sharp stroke. Certainly his work seems more convincing in the ironic rather than the epic mode. Whatever that decision, it is evident that Clarke's preoccupation—one might almost say his obsession—throughout his career has been with the power of love denied. The *persona* he turns to again and again, of either sex, of whatever time, is the one whose self-sacrificing love has been abused or diverted or simply rejected by impersonal forces. For always, even under the bitterness of his last poems, Clarke is the unquenchable romantic spirit who believes in the existence and the power of love, who can still say with his very first hero Diarmuid,

> . . . "Tell
> That as the lightning dancing on the crag
> I snatched the joy of very life from doom."
>
> [*VF* 12]

NOTES

1. Robert Farren, *The Course of Irish Verse in English* (London: Sheed and Ward, 1948), pp. 74, 130; John Montague, untitled essay, in *A Tribute to Austin Clarke on His Seventieth Birthday, 9 May 1966*, ed. John Montague and Liam Miller (Dublin: Dolmen Press, 1966), p. 9.

2. Austin Clarke, *Poetry in Modern Ireland* (Dublin: At the Three Candles Ltd. [Published for the Cultural Relations Committee of Ireland by Colm O Lochlainn], 1951), p. 42.

3. Austin Clarke, *The Vengeance of Fionn* (Dublin and London: Maunsel, 1917), p. 49. Subsequent references will be indicated parenthetically in the text by "*VF*" and the page number(s).

4. Austin Clarke, *Twice Round the Black Church: Early Memories of Ireland and England* (London: Routledge & Kegan Paul, 1962), p. 89.

5. Austin Clarke, *The Collected Poems* (London: George Allen & Unwin Ltd., 1936), p. 73. Subsequent references to poems in this edition will be indicated parenthetically in the text by *"CP"* and the page number(s).

6. Clarke, *Poetry in Modern Ireland*, p. 41.

7. Daniel Corkery, *The Hidden Ireland: A Study of Gaelic Munster in the Eighteenth Century* (Dublin: H. M. Gill and Son, 1925), pp. 129–30.

8. Clarke, *Poetry in Modern Ireland*, p. 43.

9. Austin Clarke, *Later Poems* (Dublin: Dolmen Press, 1961), p. 25. Subsequent references to poems in *Pilgrimage, Night and Morning,* and *Ancient Lights* are from this edition, and are indicated parenthetically in the text by *"LP"* and the page number(s).

10. David H. Greene, ed., *An Anthology of Irish Literature* (New York: Random House [Modern Library], 1954, pp. 28, 29, 31.

11. Thomas Kinsella, *"Magnanimity,"* in *Tribute to Austin Clarke,* p. 8; Denis Donoghue, "One More Brevity," in *Tribute to Austin Clarke,* p. 21.

12. Clarke, *Twice Round the Black Church,* p. 164.

13. Austin Clarke, *Flight to Africa and Other Poems* (Dublin: Dolmen Press, 1963), p. 45. Subsequent references to poems in this edition will be indicated parenthetically in the text by *"FA"* and the page number(s).

14. John Rees Moore, "Now Yeats Has Gone: Three Irish Poets," *Hollins Critic* 3, no. 2 (1966): 7.

15. Clarke, *Twice Round the Black Church,* p. 18.

16. Christopher Ricks, untitled essay, in *Tribute to Austin Clarke,* p. 19.

Yeats's Apocalyptic Horsemen
By Edward Hirsch

> Even the wisest man grows tense
> With some sort of violence
> "Under Ben Bulben"

In the final, haunting poem of "Nineteen Hundred and Nineteen" Herodias's daughters ride wildly through the wind. The abrupt and terrifying appearance of the daughters of Herodias represents one of Yeats's most sinister images of the Irish Sidhe, or fairies. The daughters also illustrate Yeats's powerful use of a governing image derived from folk tradition. Pictured as blind, wild, amorous, and angry, they are a far cry from the gentle Danaan hosts who flit through some of the early poems. These fairies are both haunted and haunting, simultaneously lost and predatory. The final complex image of riders is one of Yeats's most skillful and exemplary uses of the Sidhe. An inquiry into the character of the daughters can illuminate and indeed may even be necessary to any full reading of the poem. Who are Herodias's daughters, and precisely what do they suggest, here and elsewhere in Yeats's work? The question is thrust upon us with some urgency in the climactic poem of the sequence. The sixth poem begins suddenly, violently, with a clatter of hoofbeats and a tumult of winds.

> Violence upon the roads: violence of horses;
> Some few have handsome riders, are garlanded
> On delicate sensitive ear or tossing mane,

> But wearied running round and round in their courses
> All break and vanish, and evil gathers head:
> Herodias' daughters have returned again,
> A sudden blast of dusty wind and after
> Thunder of feet, tumult of images,
> Their purpose in the labyrinth of the wind;
> And should some crazy hand dare touch a daughter
> All turn with amorous cries, or angry cries,
> According to the wind, for all are blind.[1]

Herodias's daughters are here portrayed as the jealous, blind, and crazed denizens of the Otherworld crowding in upon and riding through this world. Pushing aside the last few handsome riders, the delicate spirits riding horses garlanded with flowers, they are the supernatural emblems of an evil that has gathered its full force, the culminating spirits of a world torn apart by barbarous war. In 1919, after the atrocities of the Black and Tan Terror and the nightmare of the First World War, it seemed to Yeats that only a barbarous supernatural world could be possible. Thus, one kind of supernatural creature, "the ancient inhabitants of the country," yields to another kind of spirit, the demons that Arthur Symons calls "the eternal enemy," Herodias's daughters.[2] As Peter Ure puts it, "Even the world of phantoms . . . is in a state of degeneration."[3] There has been a displacement in the Otherworld which corresponds to the violence in this one. The sudden return of Herodias's daughters signals a complete historical breakdown and change of direction. Herodias's daughters are the dark supernatural heralds of an impending Apocalypse.

It is useful to follow the idea of the daughters of Herodias backwards and forwards in some of Yeats's other work in order to understand the full implication and meaning of this violent sexual and apocalyptic image in "Nineteen Hundred and Nineteen." This will make clear how closely Yeats's folk and mythic imagery is embedded in and reflects his apocalyptic view of history. In this way, the daughters may also be linked to two corollary images, important both to "Nineteen

Hundred and Nineteen" and within the larger context of Yeats's *oeuvre*. For Herodias's daughters are closely associated with the image and emblem of the dancer and with the destructive vision and symbol of the wind. This complex of images can be understood in terms of Yeats's conception of the mortal-immortal relationship, a relationship characterized by ambiguity. At the heart of Yeats's mature conception of the Otherworld is the idea that there is a mutual dependence and necessary antagonism between two opposite realms. Mortals need and seek spiritual knowledge (wisdom) from the Otherworld. Immortals lack physical substance (power) and require mortals to complete their tasks. "Blood and the Moon" defines the terms:

> For wisdom is the property of the dead,
> A something incompatible with life; and power,
> Like everything that has the stain of blood,
> A property of the living. . . .
>
> [*Poems* 482]

The idea that there is a necessary antagonism and an enormous cost in the meeting between mortal lover and fairy mistress stands behind the appearance of Herodias's daughters. Too often critics come to Yeats's work with vague misconceptions of the Irish fairies, and thus with an inadequate understanding of Irish folk tradition. In following through Yeats's intricate use of a group of images associated with the Irish fairies, I hope to demonstrate how rich and meaningful an event is the appearance of the daughters of Herodias. The poem also shows Yeats characteristically recreating Irish folklore in Romantic terms; for in Yeats's syncretist imagination the fairies take their place in the Romantic tradition of *la belle dame sans merci*. "Nineteen Hundred and Nineteen" is an exemplary instance of the way in which Yeats could reshape and redefine a powerful folk tradition in the interests of a visionary art.

In a note to "Nineteen Hundred and Nineteen" Yeats identified the handsome riders of the poem with the Irish fairies, or the Sidhe as they are called in Gaelic. In establishing the daughters as a darker brand or type of fairy he also notes the corespondence between the two worlds.

> The country-people see at times certain apparitions whom they name now 'fallen angels,' now 'ancient inhabitants of the country,' and describe as riding at whiles 'with flowers upon the heads of the horses.' I have assumed in the sixth poem that these horsemen, now that the times worsen, give way to worse. [*Poems* 433]

The two most common explanations of the origins of the fairies are that they are either fallen angels (too evil for heaven but too good for hell) or else that they are the old gods of the earth, the ancient inhabitants of pagan Ireland. Of the fairies it is said that some were thrown out of heaven upon the land, others into the sea, others into a whirlwind during the War of Heaven. The source of the darker spirits of the age, Herodias's daughters, is most immediately Arthur Symons's Paterian poem, "The Dance of the Daughters of Herodias." Symons marks how the daughters dance

> With their eternal, white, unfaltering feet,
> And always, when they dance, for their delight,
> Always a man's head falls because of them.
> Yet they desire not death, they would not slay
> Body or soul, no, not to do them pleasure:
> They desire love, and the desire of men;
> And they are the eternal enemy.[4]

The careful reader of Yeats would not have needed the note appended to the poem in *The Tower* (1928). Some twenty-nine years before, in a note to the poem "The Hosting of the Sidhe," Yeats had already emphasized the connection between the whirling winds, the dazzling supernatural horsemen of the Sidhe, and the medieval spirits who appear as Herodias's daughters. In 1899 Yeats wrote

Sidhe is also Gaelic for wind, and certainly the Sidhe have

much to do with the wind. They journey in whirling winds, the winds that were called the dance of the daughters of Herodias in the Middle Ages, Herodias doubtless taking the place of some old goddess. When the country people see the leaves whirling on the road they bless themselves, because they believe the Sidhe to be passing by. [*Poems* 800][5]

Two years earlier in his essay "The Tribes of Danu" Yeats had also linked the Sidhe to Herodias's daughters and then connected them to the wind. He writes: "The whirling winds that are their winds, but were called the dance of the daughters of Herodias in the middle ages, show how much their way is a whirling way."[6] The association between the Sidhe and the wind, made explicit by the Gaelic term and emphasized in many of the tales about the fairies, is capitalized on not only in "The Hosting of the Sidhe" but also in "The Host of the Air," "The Unappeasable Host," "The Secret Rose," and in the volume in which all four appear, *The Wind Among the Reeds* (1899). That title itself signifies and affirms the presence of these invisible supernatural creatures moving through the visible natural world. Yeats's idea of "the winds that were called the dance of the daughters of Herodias" also recalls Wilde's *Salomé,* and, as both Wilde's play and Symons's poem do, Mallarmé's "Hérodiade," which Yeats would have known through Symons's translation of the poem.[7]

The daughters not only travel everywhere in whirling winds; they also dance continually in them. As Yeats tells us, when the Sidhe steal humans, as all who know them know they are wont to do, "they take the good dancers too, for they love the dance."[8] Or, in the opening words of *The King of the Great Clock Tower:* "They dance all day who dance in Tir-nan-oge." Tir-nan-oge is the fairy country, the heaven of ancient peoples, the Otherworld, the "predestined dancing-place."[9] The concept of an eternal dance in that country is crucial both to Yeats's ideas about the Sidhe and, simultaneously, about the aesthetic enterprise itself.

Yeats inherited from Mallarmé (filtered through the influence of Symons and Wilde, an influence incorporated and at the same time surpassed) the symbolist idea that the dancer represents the perfect work of art. She is self-transcendent or in Yeats's word "self-begotten." In "Poet and Dancer Before Diagilev" Frank Kermode notes how for Mallarmé the American dancer Loie Fuller represented "a kind of spatial equivalent of Music."[10] In a slight but crucial modification of the Paterian formula, this becomes an emblem of the aspiration of art itself. Enigmatic, eternal, cut loose from the quotidian world, "purified," the dancer approximates what Yeats calls Unity of Being. She is also an ideal of perfect feminine beauty. This idea of the dancer is best represented by the celebrated last stanza of "Among School Children."

> Labour is blossoming or dancing where
> The body is not bruised to pleasure soul,
> Nor beauty born out of its own despair,
> Nor blear-eyed wisdom out of midnight oil.
> O chestnut-tree, great-rooted blossomer,
> Are you the leaf, the blossom or the bole?
> O body swayed to music, O brightening glance,
> How can we know the dancer from the dance?
> [*Poems* 445–46]

After Mallarmé the dancer (inseparable from the dance) becomes the exemplary image of poetry itself. In his essay, "Poésie et pensée abstraite" (1939) Paul Valéry develops one of his happiest and most famous analogies, an analogy dependent upon premises established by Mallarmé. Valéry formulates that "Walking, like prose, has a definite aim." It is instrumental. But dancing, like poetry, has no end or goal but itself. It is movement for its own sake.

> The dance is quite another matter. It is, of course, a system of actions; but of actions whose end is in themselves. It goes nowhere. If it pursues an object, it is only an ideal object, a state, an enchantment, the phantom of a flower,

an extreme of life, a smile—which forms at last on the face of the one who summoned it from empty space.[11]

This is the symbolist credo of the poem as ineffable, Platonic, unified. It is also the exemplary analogy of the poem and the dance. And that extreme of life, that moment of revelation, has deep implications for the symbolist artist.

In Yeats's terms, as developed in the tradition of Mallarmé, there is a pathological dimension to the divergent type of movement, the symbolic dance. The symbolic dance (as itself and as an emblem of the poetic endeavor) extracts a human cost. This is characteristically represented by the figure of Salome. In borrowing and transforming the Salome figure, Yeats aligns himself in a thoroughly Romantic tradition, but he localizes that cult and, as it were, grafts it onto Irish folk tradition. For Salome is necessarily affiliated in Yeats's thought with the Irish fairies. Kermode makes precisely this point in *Romantic Image* when he writes that "In Yeats's work, the notion of human sacrifice as the price of the symbolic dance is deeply and curiously embedded. From very early days he associates Salome with the sidhe."[12] One figure in particular best represents the perfect supernatural beauty and the fatal lure of the fairies: the Leanhaun Shee. This supernatural creature is clearly a kind of Salome figure.

The Leanhaun Shee is one of the gloomy and malignant solitary fairies. Like other solitary fairies, and as the name suggests, she travels alone and is seldom seen in troops. She is also, like other spirits, only half in the world of form. But the distinguishing characteristic of the Leanhaun Shee is that she is the Gaelic muse. In *Fairy and Folk Tales of the Irish Peasantry* Yeats introduces her as such:

> *The Leanhaun Shee* (fairy mistress), seeks the love of mortals. If they refuse, she must be their slave; if they consent, they are hers, and can only escape by finding another to take their place. The fairy lives on their life, and they waste away. Death is no escape from her. She is the Gaelic muse, for she gives inspiration to those she perse-

cutes. The Gaelic poets die young, for she is restless, and will not let them remain long on earth—this malignant phantom.[13]

Later in the book Yeats again writes of the artistic glory and price of the poet's fatal attraction to the predatory Sidhe. The Leanhaun Shee is the muse of Gaelic poetry, but is also the emblem of the cost to the Romantic artist. Yeats writes,

> The *Leanhaun shee* lives upon the vitals of its chosen, and they waste and die. She is of the dreadful solitary fairies. To her have belonged the greatest of the Irish poets, from Oisin down to the last century.[14]

The Leanhaun Shee is simultaneously life-giving (she gives inspiration) and life-denying (she lives off the vitals of poets). When Thomas Whitaker writes that "like Symons' daughters of Herodias, the Sidhe embody the fatal lure of immortal passion and beauty," it is the Leanhaun Shee who is most relevantly evoked.[15] It is this figure who is most likely the prototype of the Woman of the Sidhe who does the final dance in *At the Hawk's Well*. Cleena of the Wave who drives Owen Sullivan to madness and death (and his later incarnation as Hanrahan) is also of the Leanhaun Shee. Niamh, who lures Oisin into the Otherworld in "The Wanderings of Oisin," and Fand, who struggles for Cuchulain in *The Only Jealousy of Emer*, also belong to the type of the Leanhaun Shee. In fact, as Allen Grossman states in his definitive study of *The Wind Among the Reeds*, "All of Yeats's early poetic self-images were preyed upon by 'the dreadful solitary fairy,' who symbolizes the terrors of sublimation required by Wisdom." Grossman also links the Leanhaun Shee, as she was clearly linked in Yeats's work from *Cathleen Ni Houlihan* onwards, to Yeats's own personal muse, Maud Gonne, and to the nationalist incarnation of the Great Mother figure, Ireland herself, the Shan Von Voght.[16] And so it is not surprising that the characteristics of this fairy may generally be associated with Herodias's daughters. She is an Irish instance of a long nineteenth-century tradition of, to use Mario Praz's phrase, a Romantic pathology.

In the systematic correlations of *A Vision* the Sidhe belong to Phase fifteen. This is a phase of supernatural incarnation, and the creatures of this phase embody complete subjectivity and light. In a note to *The Only Jealousy of Emer,* Yeats states that "the invisible fifteenth incarnation is that of the greatest possible bodily beauty."[17] The torment of the Romantic artist is to seek too passionately for that beauty, a quest rendered impossible by the modern condition. In Eliot's famous phrase, "a dissociation of sensibility" has taken place; in Yeats's terms, "Unity of Being" appears unattainable. Yeats applies a folk term to this impossible quest when he states that the artist has been "touched" by the fairies; that is, marked, separated, isolated. In these terms Yeats parallels the peasant syndrome of being "touched" by the Sidhe to the damned role of the Romantic poet. The symbolist vision of an ape eating precious jewels in *The Celtic Twilight* becomes a similar vision of the cost to the Romantic artist. Yeats concludes,

> I knew that I saw my own Hell there, the Hell of the artist, and that all who sought after beautiful and wonderful things with too avid a thirst, lost peace and form and became shapeless and common.[18]

The dance of the Woman of the Sidhe is an emblem of the unity of mind and body, music and movement. But this reconciling image, perceived in visionary moments between sleeping and waking (the trance state necessary for the working of the creative process) is beyond reach of the modern artist. For the dance as an image of art itself, vital but distinct from life, Yeats often uses the image of the Sidhe in the special guise of Herodias's daughters, or of Herodias herself. A representative example occurs in "The Tragic Generation" where art is viewed as

> separate from everything heterogeneous and casual, from

> all character and circumstance, as some Herodiade of our theatre, dancing seemingly along in her narrow moving luminous circle.[19]

The Paterian woman who does that dance is sensuous, cruel, mysterious, detached from life, and beautiful.

In *The Romantic Agony* Mario Praz traces through the nineteenth century the tradition of the *femme fatale* or Fatal Woman (a woman of satanic beauty and sensual cruelty) and links her to the special figure of Salome. Praz's examination of the Salome figure extends from Heine's "Atta Troll" (1841) to Wilde's *Salomé* (1893) including the Salomés of Flaubert, Moreau, Laforgue, Mallarmé, and Arthur O'Shaughnessy,[20] and it is this tradition, sometimes through its decadent manifestations, to which Yeats is heir.

In his celebrated essay on Leonardo (in *The Renaissance*, 1873), Walter Pater established the outlines and fixed the character of the Fatal Woman. It was Pater who, in his discovery of her in the smile of the Gioconda, also observed her sinister aspect that he found present in all of Leonardo's work.[21] Before discussing the Mona Lisa, Pater first located, as he put it, "Leonardo's type of womanly beauty," in two small drawings, one in Florence, one in the Louvre. Pater described the women in these drawings as "Daughters of Herodias," and the character he ascribed to them—prophetic, fatal, pagan, subliminal instruments of nature—is wholly relevant to Yeats's later use of the daughters. In Pater's terms, Leonardo's daughters of Herodias are of the same family as the Gioconda. Pater laments that the originals of Leonardo's *Daughter of Herodias* and *Head of John the Baptist* have been lost, but how he himself must have imagined the subjects of those studies may be derived from the "general principles" he sees at work elsewhere in Leonardo's work. Pater's description of the Mona Lisa informs Yeats's idea of feminine beauty, of the dancer, and of the Sidhe—all of whom comprise his figure of Herodias's daughters. She is the expressive female image of "what in the ways of a thousand years men had come to desire."[22] In his introduction to *The*

Oxford Book of Modern Verse (1936), Yeats noted that Pater was the only writer to have "the entire uncritical admiration" of the younger generation. And to show the "revolutionary importance" of Pater's essay on Leonardo, he printed the celebrated passage on the Mona Lisa *vers libre*. In praise of the poem, which is a curious hybrid of Pater and Yeats, Yeats stated that Pater offered "instead of moral earnestness life lived as 'a pure gem-like flame.' "[23] This is also the character ascribed to the dancer. Yeats relied on a parallel concrete image of the Fatal Woman in his portrait of the three supernatural women who move through "The Double Vision of Michael Robartes." In Yeats's words:

> In contemplation had those three so wrought
> Upon a moment, and so stretched it out
> That they, time overthrown,
> Were dead yet flesh and bone.
>
> [*Poems* 384]

It is a similar woman, Fand, the masked Woman of the Sidhe, who is evoked in *The Only Jealousy of Emer*. An angry Emer complains

> I know her sort.
> They find our men asleep, weary with war,
> Lap them in cloudy hair or kiss their lips;
> Our men awake in ignorance of it all,
> But when we take them in our arms at night
> We cannot break their solitude.
>
> [*Plays* 549, 551]

The picture of the dancer, "dead yet flesh and bone," is the appropriate image evoked by the Herodias emblem.

Herodias of the Sidhe exists within the tradition articulated by Keats in his famous poem "La Belle Dame Sans Merci." She is the symbol of a profound, subjective, ideal beauty. She is also the Muse, the incarnation of the creature, "the white woman" who, after her appearance in "A Poet to His Beloved," becomes, as Grossman observes, the central icon of *The Wind Among the Reeds*.[24]

A Poet to His Beloved

> I bring you with reverent hands
> The books of my numberless dreams,
> White woman that passion has worn
> As the tide wears the dove-grey sands,
> And with heart more old than the horn
> That is brimmed from the pale fire of time:
> White woman with numberless dreams,
> I bring you my passionate rhyme.
>
> [*Poems* 157]

This is the same beloved who is asked in "He Bids His Beloved Be at Peace" to

> . . . let your eyes half close, and your heart beat
> Over my heart, and your hair fall over my breast,
> Drowning love's lonely hour in deep twilight of rest.
>
> [*Poems* 154]

Here the lady's hair is invoked to sexually protect and hide the poet-lover from the awkward tumult of the quotidian world. In "He Gives His Beloved Certain Rhymes" she is again asked to "Fasten your hair with a golden pin, / And bind up every wandering tress."

> You need but lift a pearl-pale hand,
> And bind up your long hair and sigh;
> And all men's hearts must burn and beat;
> And candle-like foam on the dim sand,
> And stars climbing the dew-dropping sky,
> Live but to light your passing feet.
>
> [*Poems* 158]

"He Gives His Beloved Certain Rhymes" is a particularly central lyric as it implicitly connects the white woman to the Salome figure. This becomes evident when one considers that Yeats's story "The Binding of the Hair" (January 1896) was first written as a prologue to the poem initially entitled "Aedh Gives His Beloved Certain Rhymes." In the story the bard

Aedh's head is taken off with a sword in battle and afterwards sings "a sweet tremulous song" to the queen. After the head sings "Fasten your hair with a golden pin," it is pecked by crows and rolls over to the feet of Queen Dectora, the mother of Cuchulain. This action serves as an imaginative support and backdrop to the lyric itself. Ultimately Yeats came to feel that the story lacked merit, calling it "a wretched story which . . . in the end refused to achieve itself."[25] His psychological fascination with the plot, however, remained. Indeed he returned to the plot of "The Binding of the Hair" in his two late plays, *The King of the Great Clock Tower* (1935) and its offshoot or sequel, *A Full Moon in March* (1935).

In the Gnostic tradition the white woman is also an incarnation of Sophia, the archetypal figure of Wisdom upon whom God begat the world.[26] She is also the moon-colored luminous dancer who moves in a circle of light. She is the poet's beloved Muse, and the central fact of her dance is that it requires a human sacrifice. The dancer must move with or for the severed head. The words of the Old Man in the Prologue to *The Death of Cuchulain* (1939) may stand for the use of the Salome dance everywhere in Yeats's work.

> I wanted a dance because where there are no words there is less to spoil. Emer must dance, there must be severed heads—I am old, I belong to mythology—severed heads for her to dance before. [*Plays* 1052]

The dance is the ritual event: the severed head is the human cost of that event. Yeats associated the dance of Salome with the moment of insight, the moment trembling on the edge of revelation. About this visionary association and the Salome figure *A Vision* is explicit:

> When I think of the moment before revelation I think of Salome—she, too, delicately tinted or maybe mahogany dark—dancing before Herod and receiving the Prophet's head in her indifferent hands.[27]

The dance of Salome also represented for Yeats the archaic

ritual dance that defined seasonal changes in the year in tribal societies. Yeats's anthropological contemporaries were involved in tracking the roots of dance to primitive rituals, and in the story of Salome Yeats found a hieratic emblem of the mother goddess and the slain god. Yeats's idea clearly derives from Frazer, and his vagueness in following Wilde's *Salomé* back through Heine's "Atta Troll" should not conceal the crucial source. In the preface to *A Full Moon in March* Yeats writes:

> The dance with the severed head, suggests the central idea of Wilde's *Salomé*. Wilde took it from Heine who has somewhere described Salome in hell throwing into the air the head of John the Baptist. Heine may have found it in some old Jewish religious legend for it is part of the old ritual of the year: the mother goddess and the slain god. [*Plays* 1010]

The ritual and visionary significance of the dance is that it prefigures a new era: one age dying, another about to be born.

There can be little doubt that there are strong psychosexual implications in the idea of the dancer's demanding a man's severed head—certainly a powerful castration image, indicating the fear of sexuality and the power of the algolagnic feminine figure in the tradition of *la belle dame sans merci*. In Yeats's work the Salome figure of the dancer most often appears in the guise of the Woman of the Sidhe. The idea of the Woman of the Sidhe who needs and thus steals away her mortal lover is perhaps Yeats's most crucial borrowing from folklore. There is a significant development of this idea—and of the associated motif of the journey to the Otherworld—in Yeats's work. For the moment there is only space to suggest this development in vague outline. As it first appears in Yeats's work the abduction theme is rendered sexually innocuous by dramatizing either or both the fairies and their abductee as children. This repression of the image is evident in "The Stolen Child" where the mortal who is taken is indeed a child and thus pre-sexual. In *The Land of Heart's*

Desire, the mortal is a young bride, but the immortal is a fairy child. In both cases the sexual implications of the relationship between mortal and immortal are diverted. A transitional poem in this regard is "The Hosting of the Sidhe" where the sexual threat is strongly implied both by the imagery and by the quasi-manic rhythms of the text. In later work the psychosexual implications of the theme are fully faced. In *The Only Jealousy of Emer,* Fand abducts the mortal Cuchulain from his deathbed and is indeed an incarnation of the Leanhaun Shee. She is the beautiful predatory Muse who inspires Cuchulain and would lure him into the Otherworld at the cost of his life.[28] The Queen figure at the center of "The Cap and Bells," *The King of the Great Clock Tower,* and *A Full Moon in March* belongs to the same incarnation and lineage. It is also this idea of the fatal moon goddess that stands behind the tumultuous appearance of Herodias's daughters in "Nineteen Hundred and Nineteen." In actuality, the sexual implications of the relationship between mortal and immortal take on a particularly sinister dimension at the conclusion of the poem. There the Salome figure who dances with the severed head is transformed into the image of Lady Kyteler, the witch who cohabits with "her insolent fiend," Robert Artisson. Indeed this copulation may be the revelation that the daughters of Herodias prefigure.

The moment before revelation in the poem "Nineteen Hundred and Nineteen" is the moment of an impending universal chaos. The Salome figures in the poem have one characteristic not elsewhere associated with the various women of the Sidhe in Yeats's work: they are blind. It is this blindness, this loss of control, that particularly defines the image as apocalyptic. It also links the dancer's moment of revelation to the powerful destructive wind of the poem. "The sudden blast of dusty wind" that carries the daughters into the final poem is prefigured by "those winds that clamour of approaching night" in the third poem of the sequence. It also echoes the image of sand thrown uselessly into the wind in a small poem of Blake's which Yeats called "Scoffers."

> Mock on, mock on, Voltaire, Rousseau,
> Mock on, mock on; 'tis all in vain;
> You throw the sand against the wind,
> And the wind blows it back again.[29]

The repetitive idea of mockery and the destructive frenzy of the wind may also be connected to James Clarence Mangan's poem "Gone in the Wind."

> Solomon! where is thy throne? It is gone in the wind.
> Babylon! where is thy might? It is gone in the wind.
> Like the swift shadows of Noon, like the dreams of the Blind,
> Vanish the glories and pomps of the earth in the wind.[30]

In Mangan's poem, as in Blake's Urizenic vision, nothing can survive the destructive forces of history. All vanishes in dust and wind. Thus the blind supernatural horsemen who find their only purpose "in the labyrinth of the wind" ride furiously into the winter cold of an antithetical year. The violent hoofbeat of their horses reverberates in a world facing its own blinding moment of revelation. For the wind, too, indicates that "Surely some revelation is at hand." F. A. C. Wilson defines the necessary associations of the wind:

> This wind intimates that the end of a cycle is near at hand, for this is Yeats's symbol for the destructive bouleversement that takes place at a reversal of the gyres; it is the apocalyptic "great wind of love and hate" which destroys the established world order of "The Secret Rose," and "the sudden blast of dusty wind" which (together with Yeats's equally apocalyptic horsemen) presages the final overthrow of civilization in "Nineteen Hundred and Nineteen."[31]

Early in Yeats's work the wind is, as he put it, "a symbol of vague desires and hopes" (*Poems* 806). For Yeats the wind always retained a sexual character, but by the time of *Crossways* (1889) it was already transformed in his thought into a defined region, a demon-ridden country, dreaded and malignant. In a note to *The Wind Among the Reeds,* he quoted P. W. Joyce to the effect that "Of all the different kinds of goblins . . . air demons were most dreaded by the people. They lived among clouds, and mists, and rocks, and hated the human race with the utmost malignity."[32] It is this wind that George Russell warned against in the *Irish Theosophist:* "But most of all dread the powers that move in air, their nature is desire unquenchable."[33] It is this wind that Yeats was no doubt thinking of when he remembered "I became a man, a hater of the wind . . ." ("He Thinks of His Past Greatness When a Part of the Constellations of Heaven"). It is just such a group of demons of air who ride into "Nineteen Hundred and Nineteen." And so the great wind of demonic chaos and the blind dance of Salome are successfully poured together in the form of Herodias's daughters.

In the sudden appearance of the daughters Yeats was most likely also referring to a popular legend, or some similar traditional folk story, of the goblin hunt.[34] Yeats knew that "the monstrous passion" of Wilde's Salomé ultimately derives from Heine's "Atta Troll." Heine in turn relies on the legend of a traditional cavalcade of witches on St. John the Baptist's Eve. In Heine's poem the witch Uraka describes a procession of spirits which includes Herodias. Herodias is pictured as the archetypal vampire, the original she-devil ("if a devil or an angel / I know not"). Heine rewrites the Biblical story of John the Baptist and in the exquisite irony of his imagination describes a Herodias who had once been in love with the Prophet, had demanded his head, and, once attaining it, had fallen in love with it again, consequently dying of "love's distraction." With the head in her hands she is now forced to ride in the cavalcade of witches through hell. Heine's Herodias is an image of hysteria. When combined with the caricature of the woman in Laforgue, Herodias becomes a figure, in Praz's words, "emptied of all tragic content."[35] Heine's image is wholly applicable to the hysterical riders who ride blindly into the wind of 1919. The goblin hunt is also relevant as Herodias's daughters give way to the final characters of the poem: the Irish witch Lady Kyteler and her incubus Robert Artisson.

> But now wind drops, dust settles; thereupon
> There lurches past, his great eyes without thought
> Under the shadow of stupid straw-pale locks,
> That insolent fiend Robert Artisson
> To whom the love-lorn Lady Kyteler brought
> Bronzed peacock feathers, red combs of her cocks.
> *[Poems* 433]

Alice Kyteler was an Irish woman accused of witchcraft in the fourteenth century. Her incubus was said to be Robert Artisson. In his note to "Nineteen Hundred and Nineteen" Yeats identifies him as "an evil spirit much run after in Kilkenny at the start of the fourteenth century" *(Poems* 433). Yeats read an account in the British Museum of the 1324 Inquisition against Lady Alice Kyteler, her son William, and several accomplices. Jeffares identifies two of the charges which have particular significance to the poem:

> 2. They offered in sacrifice to demons living animals, which they dismembered, and then distributed at crossroads to a certain evil spirit of low rank, named the Son of Art.
> 7. The said dame had a certain demon, an incubus, named Son of Art, or Robin son of Art, who had carnal knowledge of her, and from whom she admitted that she had received her wealth. This incubus made its appearance under various forms, sometimes as a cat, or as a hairy black dog, or in the likeness of a negro (Ethiops), accompanied by two others who were larger and taller than he, and of whom one carried an iron rod.[36]

In his account of the proceedings, Yeats's contemporary W. G. Wood-Martin also recalls how Dame Kyteler "had sacrificed to him at a certain stone bridge, nine red cocks, and nine peacocks' eyes; and on more than one occasion she had anointed a red coulter and performed long aerial journeys on it."[37] Yeats himself remembers the sacrifice in his notes to *Visions and Beliefs in the West of Ireland.* What is stated definitely in the poem is posed, in those notes, as a question.

> Did Dame Kettler, a great lady of Kilkenny who was accused of witchcraft early in the fifteenth century, find such a lover when she offered up the combs of cocks and the bronzed tail feathers of nine peacocks; or had she indeed, as her enemies affirmed at the trial, been enamoured with "one of the meaner sort of hell"?[38]

Yeats's designation of Artisson as an "insolent fiend" would seem to indicate that, for the rhetorical purposes of the poem, Lady Kyteler was indeed enamored with "one of the meaner sort of hell."

Robert Artisson may be considered, as Yeats himself suggested in *Visions and Beliefs,* one of the Sidhe, a malignant spirit of the Otherworld, the description of his "stupid straw-pale locks" recalls Symons's characterization of the daughters as ignorant: "For they are stupid, and they do not know/ That they are slaying the messenger of God."[39] The most repulsive traits of the daughters are embodied in the figure of Artisson. And the human cost, the human complicity in the barbarism is represented by the carnal knowledge and witchcraft of Lady Kyteler. Whitaker calls her "virtually a human daughter of Herodias," for in the accounts against her it was said that Lady Kyteler was one of the witches called out at night by a spirit known as Herodias.[40]

When called out, she longs to copulate with her sordid spectral lover. The coxcomb (with its blatant sexual pun) that the "love-lorn" Lady Kyteler brings to her spirit lover is an explicit genital symbol, an overt sexual offering. And the Irish witch's cohabitation with the Son of Art is a degrading and repulsive parody and reversal of the poet's relationship to the Muse. This is what the times have come to. The barbarism of the supernatural world is evoked and matched by the barbarism of the human world. The revelation is at hand.

In the final poem of "Nineteen Hundred and Nineteen," Yeats needed a symbol energetic and forceful enough to suggest a universal Apocalypse. He found in Herodias's daughters a single condensed image with a range of violent but controlled associations. He energized a folk image with a range of personal and Romantic associations and, in the process, wholly transformed it. In his essay on Leonardo, Pater suggested that Leonardo's problem was "the transmutation of ideas into images."[41] This is perhaps the problem of all Romantic artists who, as it is put in "Ego Dominus Tuus," "seek an image, not a book." In the character of the Sidhe as they appear in the special guise of Herodias's daughters, Yeats found a rich image equal to the demands made of it by his complex, visionary intellect.

NOTES

1. The poem, written in 1919, was originally entitled "Thoughts upon the Present State of the World" and appeared in *The Dial* 71 (September 1921): 265–69 and *The London Mercury* 5 (November 1921): 7–10. The title was changed when the poem was collected in *The Tower* (1928).

2. See Yeats's note after the text in *The Variorum Edition of the Poems of W. B. Yeats*, ed. Peter Allt and Russell K. Alspach (New York: Macmillan Co., 1957), p. 433. Hereafter cited parenthetically in the text as *Poems*. See also Arthur Symons's *Poems*, 2 vols. (New York: John Lane Co., 1909), 2: 105.

3. Peter Ure, *Towards a Mythology: Studies in the Poetry of W. B. Yeats* (1946; New York: Russell and Russell, 1967), p. 71.

4. Symons's poem first appeared in *Images of Good and Evil* (1899) and was collected in *Poems*, 2: 103–7; see especially p. 105.

5. John Vickery, in *The Literary Impact of "The Golden Bough"* (Princeton, N.J.: Princeton University Press, 1973), p. 187, notes the influence of Frazer in Yeats's substitution of Herodias for some old goddess. He writes, "this substitution of one figure for another as mythology adapts to varying historical and cultural circumstances is an integral part of *The Golden Bough*." In associating the Sidhe and the wind Yeats was relying on common folk knowledge. Sean O'Súilleabháin, in *A Handbook of Irish Folklore* (1942; Detroit, Mich.: Singing Tree Press, 1970), p. 477, says, "sudden or unusual blasts of wind, especially whirlwinds on a summer day, were popularly associated with the fairies." Yeats also writes, in his *Uncollected Prose*, 2 vols. ed. John P. Frayne and Colin Johnson (New York: Columbia University Press, 1975), 2: 76, "the number of those whose cries are heard in the wind shows how much 'the others' have to do with the wind."

6. Yeats, *Uncollected Prose*, 2: 69.

7. See Arthur Symons's *Poems*, 1: 205–7.
8. Yeats, *Uncollected Prose*, 2: 81.
9. In the sixth poem, "Her Courage," in "Upon a Dying Lady," Yeats anticipates Mabel Beardsley's death:

> When her soul flies to the predestined dancing-place
> (I have no speech but symbol, the pagan speech I made
> Amid the dreams of youth). . . .
>
> [*Poems* 365–66]

Vickery argues that Yeats's idea of a predestined dancing place owes something to Frazer's account of "dancing's forming 'a conspicuous feature of the great festival of the dead' so that 'the festival which began so lugubriously ends by being the merriest of the year.'" *The Literary Impact of "The Golden Bough"* pp. 198–99. It is perhaps more likely that Yeats derived it from Alfred Nutt's *Celtic Otherworld*.

10. Frank Kermode, "Poet and Dancer Before Diagilev," *Partisan Review* 28 (January-February 1961): 70.
11. "Poésie et pensée abstraite" was first delivered as a lecture at Oxford, 1 March 1939 and subsequently published by the Clarendon Press, 1939. See Paul Valéry's *The Art of Poetry*, trans. Denise Folliot, in *The Collected Works of Paul Valéry*, ed. Jackson Mathews, 15 vols. (New York: Pantheon, 1958), 7:70.
12. Frank Kermode, *Romantic Image* (1957; London: Routledge and Kegan Paul, 1976), p. 89.
13. W. B. Yeats, ed, *Fairy and Folk Tales of the Irish Peasantry*, 1918; rptd. as *Fairy and Folk Tales of Ireland* (New York: Boni and Liveright, 1979), p. 86.
14. Ibid., p. 156.
15. Thomas Whitaker, *Swan and Shadow: Yeats's Dialogue with History* (Chapel Hill, N.C.: University of North Carolina Press, 1964), p. 230.
16. Allen R. Grossman, *Poetic Knowledge in the Early Yeats: A Study of "The Wind Among the Reeds"* (Charlottesville, Va: University of Virginia Press, 1969), p. 38.
17. *The Variorum Edition of the Plays of W. B. Yeats*, ed. Russell K. Alspach (London: Macmillan and Co., 1966), p. 566. Hereafter cited parenthetically in the text as *Plays*.
18. W. B. Yeats, *Mythologies* (New York; Macmillan Co., 1959), p. 100.
19. *The Autobiography of William Butler Yeats* (1938; New York: Macmillan Co., 1971), p. 193.
20. Mario Praz, *The Romantic Agony* (1933: Oxford University Press, 1970), p. 253.
21. Walter Pater, *The Renaissance: Studies in Art and Poetry* (1873; London: Macmillan and Co., 1919), p. 124. In an early vision of *A Vision*, Yeats also discussed the nature of the woman who "desires so little and gives so little that men will die and murder in her service." See *A Critical Edition of Yeats's "A Vision" (1925)*, ed. George Mills Harper and Walter Kelly Hood (London: Macmillan and Co., 1978), p. 68.
22. Pater, *The Renaissance*, p. 124.
23. *The Oxford Book of Modern Verse, 1892–1935*, chosen by W. B. Yeats (New York: Oxford University Press, 1936), p. ix.
24. Grossman, *Poetic Knowledge*, p. 21.
25. Yeats to Edmond Gosse, 23 November 1895, in *The Letters of W. B. Yeats*, ed. Allan Wade (New York: Macmillan Co., 1955), p. 258. The story was printed in

the 1897 edition of *The Secret Rose*, but after 1908 it was dropped and never reprinted. It may be found in *Uncollected Prose*, 1: 390–93.

26. See Grossman, *Poetic Knowledge*, p. 21. Yeats would have known of Sophia's place in the Kabbalistic system through S. L. MacGregor Mathers, *The Kabbalah Unveiled* (London: George Redway, 1887).

27. W. B. Yeats, *A Vision* (London: Macmillan and Co., 1937), p. 273. An early version of *A Vision* was being composed at the same time as "Nineteen Hundred and Nineteen."

28. Fand is also a Maud Gonne figure. See Harper and Hood, *A Critical Edition of Yeats's "A Vision" (1925)*, p. 78.

29. See Edwin Ellis's and W. B. Yeats's edition of *The Works of William Blake* (1893; New York: AMS Press, 1973), p. 70.

30. *Selected Poems of James Clarence Mangan*, ed. Michael Smith (Dublin: Gallery Press, 1974), p. 70. See also A. Norman Jeffares, *W. B. Yeats: Man and Poet* (New Haven, Ct.: Yale University Press, 1949), pp. 224–25.

31. F. A. C. Wilson, *W. B. Yeats and Tradition* (London: Victor Gollancz, 1958), p. 228.

32. Quoted by Grossman in *Poetic Knowledge*, p. 61. Grossman tracks the Joyce source to "Fergus O'Mara and the Demons," in *Good and Pleasant Reading* (1886).

33. George Russell, "A Priestess of the Woods," *Irish Theosophist* 1 (July 1893): 99.

34. See Daniel Hoffman, *Barbarous Knowledge: Myth in the Poetry of Yeats, Graves, and Muir* (New York: Oxford University Press, 1967), pp. 72, 75–77. A. Norman Jeffares, *A Commentary on the Collected Poems of W. B. Yeats* (London: Macmillan and Co., 1968), p. 279.

35. Praz, *The Romantic Agony*, p. 316. For the German text of "Atta Troll: Ein Sommernachstraum," see *Heinrich Heines Werke* (Vienna et al.: Zweiter Band, n.d.), pp. 390ff.

36. Jeffares, *A Commentary*, p. 281.

37. W. G. Wood-Martin, *Traces of the Elder Faiths of Ireland* (1902; Port Washington, N.Y.: Kennikat Press, 1970), p. 174.

38. W. B. Yeats, in Lady Gregory's *Visions and Beliefs in the West of Ireland* (1920; Gerrards Cross: Colin Smythe, 1970), p. 344.

39. Symons, *Poems* 2:103.

40. Whitaker, *Swan and Shadow*, p. 231.

41. Pater, *The Renaissance*, p. 112.

Maud Gonne Macbride: Violent Pacifist
By Conrad A. Balliet

"I have always hated war and am by nature and philosophy a pacifist." Thus has Maud Gonne described herself in her autobiographical *A Servant of the Queen*. Yet she wrote in the same book that she wanted the evicted tenants to "Shoot the Landlords."[1] These contradictory statements are typical of that enigmatic woman, the beloved of the poet W. B. Yeats. There are similar contrasts between her writings as an old woman and her speeches as a young leader, between her public and her private statements, and between her words and her actions. It is my intent to note these contrasts and to draw some conclusions about the peaceful and the violent in the life of Maud Gonne.

There are various records of what Maud said and did in her earlier years. In addition to her often unreliable autobiography, newspapers and the Irish constabulary reported on her speeches and demonstrations. The police would have looked for dangerous, treasonable, and seditious statements. Their records include a quotation from a speech she gave at Waterford on 27 May 1896: "Why were John Daly and others in prison? Because they loved Ireland, and struck a blow at the chains that bound her. (cheers) The English might call them criminals, dynamitards if they liked, but Irishmen looked upon them as martyrs and patriots. (cheers)."[2] She did not actually incite violence in that speech, but merely admired it. A speech in Tipperary on 27 September 1896 had a similar ring: "These men could not bear the sight of Ireland lying prostrate at the feet of England, and so they went forward—madly if you will, but still heroically, to strike a blow for their country" (CO 904 20). As revolutionary rhetoric goes, the words are not very strong, and these excerpts would represent the most radical statements the police could have found. By 1901, her language had become stronger. On 8 September during the unveiling of a memorial to John Lavin at Castlerea, she told the people to "practice shooting, so that when the next opportunity for using firearms arrived they would not be found unprepared like last year." However, the Chief Crown Solicitor and the Attorney General "thought Miss Gonne's speech not quite so bad as many she had delivered, and they did not think it would be expedient to take any notice of it" (CO 903 71).

United Ireland for 7 October 1893 reported a speech at Limerick on behalf of the prisoner John Daly: "'What true Irishman,' demanded Miss Gonne, 'would dare to say to Mrs. Daly, "Do not ask for your son's release, because Mr. Gladstone is going to get Home Rule for us—some day—and the request might embarrass him?" What would the true Irishman do? He would endeavor by all means to bring pressure on the Government and force from them that act of justice or mercy without which Home Rule would not be the herald of peace from England to Ireland.'" She does not suggest any specific means of bringing pressure.

An article on "The Boer Women" in a supplement to the *United Irishman* for 10 March 1900 reveals some of her attitudes toward women as well as toward violence:

> There are two types of the Boer woman. One has known hardships always; she has lived in solitude; she knows but little of the world that lies beyond the dreary stretches of the veldt. The daughters have been content to follow the flocks of sheep and the oxen herds of their fathers, the mothers to perform the simple duties of the farm house. . . . The other type of Boer woman is the product of the cities. . . . She speaks several languages. She plays the piano, she dresses in the prevailing fashion, she dances

well. . . . She is in many respects a young woman of progressive and modern ideas.

But the difference between her and her sister is merely a thin veneer of civilisation. At heart they are the same. And each is religious, each loves her country better than her life. . . . Each of them has been taught two things—to use her Bible and her pistol. In her hour of need she trusts in both of these. . . . Disdaining a saddle she rides all day by the side of her brother, and uses rifle or pistol with the skill of a sharpshooter.

To support the Irish brigade in the Boer War and her activities on behalf of evicted tenants, Maud Gonne made three lecture tours of the U.S. around the turn of the century. She continued to preach violence as well. According to the Peoria *Evening Times* for 4 December 1897, "Miss Gonne wears a bullet attached to a charm, which was picked up on the battlefield at Castlebar, a scene of one of the Irish Nationalist victories." In her speech at Peoria, she contrasted peace and war, life and death: "Human life is very precious and should not lightly be risked, but there are some sorts of economy which are shortsighted. . . . It seems to me that constant revolution and consequent bloodshed might have proved less deadly to Ireland than all these years of peaceful ruin. A little blood makes a great stain."

On her 1900 lecture tour of America, she solicited funds both for the Amnesty Association in Ireland and for an "ambulance corps" for South Africa. The Omaha Evening *World Herald,* on 28 February 1900, reported some doubts about the purpose of the money for ambulances. "At the suggestion that the members of the ambulance corps might develop into full-fledged warriors upon arrival in the Transvaal, Miss Gonne smiled, 'I never say anything about the detachments that have gone there until I am sure they have arrived,' she said evasively." She was willing to use an appeal to mercy as a guise for supporting the war.

She also knew how to speak with a typical nineteenth century rhetorical flair. The New York *Irish World* quoted from her speech on Saturday, 10 February 1900:

> English methods of warfare have not changed since she turned loose the red savages armed with scalping knife and tomahawk to make savage war on the American colonists. To Ireland I say that freedom is never won without the sacrifice of blood. Our chance is coming. The end of the British empire is at hand. Your motherland calls you.

The paper reported that "thunders of applause greeted the close of Miss Gonne's address." Her call for the shedding of blood echoes John Mitchell and anticipates Padraic Pearse. These police and newspaper accounts show the young Maud speaking to the public at the turn of the century in strong but rather vague and general terms about violence.

The early 1900s were an interim period when Maud was less active politically—she feared returning to Ireland because of a conflict with John MacBride over custody of their son Sean, and she had to cope with the violence of World War I. At that time, in her personal letters, Maud reveals a very different attitude. The French authorities had asked her to serve as a nurse for wounded soldiers, and she experienced firsthand the effects of war. Her sister Kathleen had a son killed. On 22 April 1915, Maud wrote to John Quinn:

> We were all rather upset by the death of a dear nephew killed at Neuve Chapelle and I had to go to take care of my sister as we were afraid the shock would kill her. He was such a beautiful boy only 21. This war is dreadful. All the best, all the strongest are being killed. It is race suicide. Every kilometer of advance means the loss of about 30,000 to the attacking army and about half that to the defenders. Poor France.[3]

In several letters to "Willie," now available in the recently published *Letters to W. B. Yeats,* Maud reacts even more personally:

My dear Willie
  You seem to have escaped the obsession of this war—I cannot; night and day I think about it *uselessly*. I cannot

work, I cannot read, I cannot sleep—I am torn in two, my love of France on one side, my love of Ireland on the other. . . .

This war is an inconceivable madness which has taken hold of Europe—It is unlike any other war that has ever been. It has no great idea behind it.[4]

She says that neither the leaders nor the people know why they are fighting, except for England, who "as usual is following her commercial selfishness getting others to fight." She has vague hopes that women will help end the war:

Could the women, who are after all the guardians of the race, end it? Soon they will be in a terrible majority, unless famine destroys them too. I always felt the wave of the woman's power was rising, the men are destroying themselves and we are looking on.

Again, a few weeks later, she wrote to Willie.

I am nursing the wounded from 6 in the morning till 8 at night and trying in material work to drown the sorrow and disappointment of it all—and in my heart is growing up a wild hatred of the war machine which is grinding the life out of these great natures and reducing their population to helpless slavery and ruin.[5]

Further evidence in support of Maud as pacifist comes from relatives and friends of the MacBride family familiar with life at Roebuck House in Dublin where Maud lived from about 1923 until her death in 1953. At various times during the 1920s and 1930s, many people lived there for shorter or longer periods: Madame Despard; Helen Moloney; Maud's daughter Iseult, her husband Francis Stuart, and their two children, Kay and Ian; Sean MacBride, his wife Catalina, and their two children, Anna and Tiernan; a niece of Catalina; a full time secretary for Sean; his former governess Barry O'Delaney; and a French cook, Josephine (who spoke very little English). In addition to these, there were a host of visitors ranging from IRA members to personal friends. There are accounts of grandchildren crawling over Maud's bed—she seldom got up until the afternoon in the 1930s—and of their playing tricks on her and the guests. Yet Maud seldom became angry with relatives or friends—she expressed her anger only at the English and on political issues.[6] Her attitude helps resolve the paradox of the sentence that opens this article, a "but" sentence: "I have always hated war and am by nature and philosophy a pacifist, but it is the English who are forcing war on us, and the first principle of war is to kill the enemy" (SQ 115).

Because of her belief that the Irish needed to make constant war on England and in spite of her own repugnance at the horrors of World War I, when she returned to Ireland in 1917 she resumed her inflammatory speaking and public demonstrations, mostly on behalf of Irish prisoners. She staunchly opposed the Treaty of 1921, and Roebuck House was a center of IRA activity during the "troubles." In the 1920s and on into the 1930s she was a familiar figure on the streetcorners of Dublin, making speeches and carrying placards.[7]

By the time she came to write her autobiography in the late 1930s, her language had become even stronger, and her memories—or imaginative re-creation—of her youth present her in her most dramatic and violent moods. She recalls that Lucien Millevoye purchased a revolver for her, telling her that "No woman should ever travel without a revolver" (SQ 67). A few pages later she describes an incident with some Greek men on a rowboat when she saved herself from kidnapping by aiming the revolver and threatening the men. In another incident she challenged a nefarious editor to a duel in a Parisian shooting gallery and put her three shots through the heart of a cardboard figure, winning the duel. "Hé, Mademoiselle, I wouldn't like to fight a duel with you," one of the journalists said, according to her story, and she heard another say as she left, "Mais elle est terrible, la belle Irlandaise" (SQ 212). During a discussion of the evictions, a young Bishop O'Donnell asked about the tenants, "What can they do with the force that is against them?" "Shoot the landlords," she remembers thinking, but Maud kept silent and felt cowardly (*SQ* 106). At the evictions on the Olpherts estates, she writes, someone had taken poison from the "Cow Doctor" and put it in the drink. For a time they had thought he had died, but he had just become very sick. "I knew I hoped he would die," Maud writes, "and if I could have done anything to contribute to this death I would have done so and would have felt I was committing no sin, since he was an essential cog in the British war machine" (*SQ* 115). She claims that Parnell failed because "he repudiated acts of violence" (*SQ* 174); she approves the use of dynamite in random violence: "My friends, the Irish revolutionists may have been arranging a little dynamite plot in England,—more power to them!" (*SQ* 183); she describes her part in a plan to sink a British troopship" (*SQ* 303–05); and she believes if there were more murders like those in Phoenix Park, if "every Chief Secretary or Lord Lieutenant (or better still, every English king) were shot one after the other, Ireland would soon be free with small sacrifice of life" (*SQ* 347). These comments written around 1938 are, for the most part, more vehement than anything the police or newspapers reported her saying at the time the events occurred.

In another passage of her autobiography, she shows reluctance to follow her own advice about the shedding of blood. Two of her anti-English plots had gone awry because of the duplicity of an informer, who had been caught. Maud writes that she agreed with Father Cavanagh, whom she quotes as saying, "The only logical way to deal with spies and traitors . . . when you have no prison in which to shut them, is to shoot them as an example." She adds, "Undoubtedly the traitor deserved a bullet," but notes that she had not wanted to shoot the informer herself:

> I had made it a rule of life never to ask any man to do a thing I was not ready to do myself or to take a risk I was not ready to share. I was not ready to shoot this man. I always carried my little revolver with me and on two other occasions it had protected me since the evening on the

Greek sea where it had enabled me to catch my boat to Constantinople; but I had never fired it at any human being and I would have disliked doing so extremely. [SQ 313]

Here is a further contrast, picked up by a newspaper reporter as early as 1900: "It won't do to call her Joan of Arc, though, because Jeanne rode a horse in battle and fought hand in hand, sword to sword, with the English who burnt her alive when they caught her. Maud will probably never shoot an English man and will never be burnt alive."[8]

Her claim never to have asked others to take a risk she would not share is a dubious one. She did crawl "on a wagonette to scream" and, albeit in vague terms, she suggested violence and was involved in planning and leading activities that resulted in bloodshed and death. She helped organize a counter-demonstration at the time of the celebration of the Queen's Jubilee, and a woman demonstrator was killed on 30 June 1897. Maud, of course, blamed the English. At the time of a visit to Edward VII in 1903, she led a group to challenge the plans of Tim Harrington, and a bloody melee followed; she calls the chapter of her autobiography describing that incident, "The Battle of the Rotunda." In general, her words were more violent than her actions; she wrote more vehemently as old Madame MacBride than she spoke as the young demagogue Maud Gonne; it is likely that some of her speeches led other people to violent action.

A novel published shortly after those events of 1903 illustrates Maud's public image as an instigator of violent action and hatred.[9] The title of the book is the name of the hero, *Hyacinth*, and it is the story of a young man from the west of Ireland who finds his way to the big city of Dublin, and there comes under the sway of a Miss Goold, also known as the "famous Finola," tall, beautiful, charming, and a chain smoker of cigarettes—obviously Maud Gonne (*H* 42). The young and tender Hyacinth listens to an argument between Finola and one Tim Halloran. Tim fears they will have trouble recruiting Irishmen for the Boers, since many young

Irish are already in the English army. "'Well, then, the Irish troops ought to shoot their officers, and walk over to the Boer camp,' said Finola savagely" (*H* 47). Hyacinth takes that as a monstrous jest, and calls it "devilish treachery."

> Augusta Goold flung her cigarette into the grate, and rose from her chair. She stood over Hyacinth, her hands clenched and her bosom heaving rapidly. Her eyes blazed down into his until their scorn cowed him.
> "There is no treachery possible for an Irishman," she said, "except the one of fighting for England. Any deed against England—yes, *any* deed—is glorious, and not shameful." [*H* 48]

The young man is so moved that he decides to enlist forthwith. Another account is clearly based on the Rotunda incident in which Maud challenged Tim Harrington. The young Hyacinth comes to her rescue by hitting a protestor named Shea on the head with a stone, almost killing him. When an editorial position opens up on the *Croppy* (apparently *United Ireland*), Finola recommends Hyacinth, because he "had volunteered to fight for the Boers . . . and nearly killed that blackguard Shea" (*H* 249). She thinks he will meet the primary requirement for the position: a deep, lasting and intense hatred for "England and the Empire, and everything English, from Parliament to the police barrack . . . It is this hatred which must animate the work" (*H* 249). Eventually, after a scene with his beloved Marion and a devoted Canon, the young Hyacinth is forced to choose: the "gospel of hate," preached and embodied by Miss Goold, or the "gospel of love," preached by the Canon and embodied by "Him," that is, Christ (*H* 264–67). The scenes are melodramatic, the language overwrought, and the portrait exaggerated, but Maud obviously impressed one young man as the epitome of hate and violence. Hyacinth chose Love.

"Willie" Yeats, in his poetry, presents a similar image of Maud, and the words "violence" and "hatred" recur in his poems about her, linking violent acts with the idea of hatred:

> Why should I blame her that she filled my days
> With misery, or that she would of late
> Have taught to ignorant men most violent ways,
> Or hurled the little streets upon the great.[10]

In "Prayer for My Daughter" he asks that his daughter not resemble Maud:

> . . . to be choked with hate
> May well be of all evil chances chief.
> ....
> An intellectual hatred is the worst
> ....
> Have I not seen the loveliest woman born
> Out of the mouth of Plenty's horn,
> Because of her opinionated mind
> Barter that horn . . . .
>
> [*Poems* 185–87]

In "The Circus Animals' Desertion" he recalls Maud's youth:

> I thought my dear must her own soul destroy,
> So did fanaticism and hate enslave it.
>
> [*Poems* 335–37]

It is not hate in and of itself to which the poet objects. In "Ribh Considers Christian Love Insufficient" (*Poems* 284), Yeats through one of his numerous masks claims to "study hatred with great diligence," and he refers, in "The Fisherman" (*Poems* 145–46), to "The living men that I hate." His, however, is a "passionate," not an "intellectual" hatred. In this context, Yeats could not have meant "intellectual" in the sense of "rational" or "intelligent"—neither he nor any of the critics have accused Maud of being an "intellectual"—but in the sense of "abstract."[11] This difference between "passionate" and "intellectual" is a significant and valid one. Often in *A Servant of the Queen* and sometimes in her speeches, the scenes that Maud describes have an abstract quality and give a dramatic impression—almost like one of the *tableaux vivants* presented by Maud and her Daughters of Erin. The confrontation with the Greek oarsman or with the landlords, the challenge in a shooting gallery, the Boer woman riding with her rifle—these leave an impression very different from the wounded soldiers described in her letters to Quinn and Yeats. The focus of the public Maud is not on the individuals or their suffering, but on the message, on the English, and on the abstract cause of Irish freedom. The suffering and the violence all seem grist for the mill of her propaganda machine.

There is no doubt about the intense suffering of the evicted tenants or of the Irish prisoners in English jails. There is no doubt that the cause of Irish freedom was a worthy one. There is no doubt that Maud Gonne did admirable work in alleviating the suffering of the individual tenants, prisoners, and their families—newspapers, biographers, and children of the families have documented her achievement and the gratitude of those she helped. What is less admirable is her willingness to distort and to exploit that suffering for the purposes of her propaganda and to be insufficiently aware of the consequences of her rhetoric. Her friend W. B. Yeats, though less political, nonetheless questioned those consequences. His play *Cathleen ni Houlihan,* written for Maud, links the poet and the politician, for she played the lead role in the premier in 1902. During 1938, the year when Maud published *A Servant of the Queen* and a year before his own death, the poet still pondered the meaning of his words and their effect:

> All that I have said and done,
> Now that I am old and ill,
> Turns into a question till
> I lie awake night after night
> And never get the answers right.
> Did that play of mine send out
> Certain men the English shot?[12]

Actually, he had questioned his responsibility as early as 1916 when he wrote to John Quinn, "I keep going over the past in my mind and wondering if I could have done anything to turn those young men in another direction."[13] Though Maud had written to Willie that she lay awake thinking about the horrors of World War I, she does not seem to have lost any sleep over the wisdom of her own words that urged and occasionally led to violent action. And the conjecture of the newspaper reporter in 1900 was correct: the Irish Joan of Arc was not burned at the stake and she shot no Englishmen. She died of cardiac failure at the age of 86, and the only record of her shooting any living creature is her own account in *A Servant of the Queen* of killing a lark: "I was overwhelmed with the horror of my deed" (*SQ* 147).

Whether ultimately her political words and acts or the poetry of Willie Yeats contributed more to Irish freedom is a question that remains to be answered. There stands now an image of a woman—peaceful, sensitive, concerned, tolerant, lovable to those closest to her, who felt in herself an intense hatred and who with strong speech evoked a similar hatred in others—a violent pacifist.

NOTES

1. Maud Gonne MacBride, *A Servant of the Queen* (London: Gollancz, 1938), pp. 106, 115. All page references to this edition are hereafter cited parenthetically in the text with the abbreviation *SQ*.

2. London Public Records Office, Colonial Office Files: CO 904 20. Subsequent references are cited parenthetically with the abbreviation CO.

3. Maud Gonne to John Quinn, 22 April 1915, John Quinn Collection, New York Public Library, N.Y.

4. Maud Gonne to W. B. Yeats, 26 August 1914, *Letters to W. B. Yeats*, ed. Richard Finneran et al., 2 vols. (New York: Columbia University Press, 1977), 2:303.

5. Gonne to Yeats, 7 November 1914, *Letters*, 2:308.

6. This information comes from interviews I have had during the summers of 1974–77 while doing research towards a biography of Maud Gonne. I have talked with Francis and Kay Stuart, Sean MacBride, the late Mrs. "Kid" MacBride, and Mrs. Louie O'Brien (Sean's former secretary). Their answer to my repeated question, "Did you ever see Madame angry?" were consistently, "only at the English," "only on political issues," or words to that effect.

7. Her activities during this period have been documented by a number of writers, including Samuel Levenson, *Maud Gonne* (New York: Reader's Digest Press, 1976), and Nancy Cardozo, *Lucky Eyes and a High Heart: The Life of Maud Gonne* (New York: Bobbs-Merrill, 1978).

8. The quotation is from the New York *Catholic Weekly Union*, 10 February 1900. During my interviews in Dublin in 1975 I talked with an old man, a prominent Irishman who prefers not to be identified, who repeated a similar view: "I do not like what I know about Maud, or her son Sean for that matter. Both are willing to urge others to violence, causing them to get injured or killed, while they themselves run very few risks."

9. The novel, published under the pseudonym of George A. Birmingham, was by James O. Hannay: *Hyacinth* (London: Edward Arnold, 1906). All page references to his edition are hereafter cited in the text with the abbreviation *H*. In *Letters to W. B. Yeats*, 1:180, there is a letter from Maud dated April 1907, in which she writes: "My dear Willie, all this time I have not written to thank you for sending me *Hyacinth*." The editors conjecture that the reference was to Yeats's *Hyacinth Halvey;* it is more likely that he sent Maud the novel about herself.

10. "No Second Troy," in *The Collected Poems of W. B. Yeats* (New York: Macmillan Co., 1956), p. 89. All page references to this edition are hereafter cited parenthetically in the text with the shortened title *Poems*.

11. In another poem, "Blood and the Moon," Yeats refers to fanatics who have killed "out of an abstract hatred" *(Poems* 232–34).

12. The poem quoted is "The Man and the Echo" *(Poems* 377).

13. Yeats to John Quinn, 23 May 1916, in *The Letters of W. B. Yeats*, ed. Allan Wade (New York: Macmillan Co., 1955), p. 614. William Irwin Thompson, in his study *The Imagination of an Insurrection: Dublin Easter 1916* (New York: Harper Colophon Books, 1967) notes the complexities of these issues and concludes, "Cathleen ni Houlihan did send out certain men to be shot, but many things had placed them in a frame of mind to be sent out, and these were the very things that had placed Yeats in a frame of mind to write the play" (233).

The Presence of Parnell in Three Plays by Lady Gregory
By Benilde Montgomery

There is little doubt that Lady Gregory was "single-mindedly a rebel nationalist."[1] Unlike Yeats, she committed herself to Republicanism during the Civil War, and although Lennox Robinson's report[2] of her public defiance of Black-and-Tan bullets recalls an indecorous extreme, it is, nonetheless, consistent with a preoccupation with Home Rule and the re-establishment of Ireland's political integrity that a study of her journals reveals. The shape of her nationalism, moreover, was in large measure determined by her devotion to the personality and cause of Charles Stewart Parnell. We know, for example, that when he died in October 1891, she tore an account of his funeral from a newspaper and stored it among her personal papers. With it she kept Katherine Tynan's lament for the dead Chief:

> Tonight and many a night in restless slumber
>   Shall dream you are not dead
> And wake to weep sick tears without number
>   O'er your beloved head.

When Lady Gregory herself died in 1932, among the drawings and sketches found in her study at Coole was one of Parnell's last photographs. Across the back of it, she had copied from an old ballad:

> Oh, I have dreamed a dreamy dream
> Beyond the isle of Skye

> I saw a dead man win a fight
> And I think that man was I.

Yet for all her devotion to Parnell, there are remarkably few direct references to him in her published works. His name is mentioned in only one of her plays—*The Image;* it is glossed over in Robinson's haphazard edition of her *Journals;* it appears only with passing interest in her *Autobiography;* and, while it appears with some regularity in Daniel J. Murphy's splendid edition of the *Journals* (1978), it never becomes the focus of sustained argument.[3]

Nonetheless, she tells us that her nationalism was far more profound "than they know or my nearest realised."[4] The necessity for a clandestine approach to her rebel hero is explicable for many reasons, the dictates of her own class not being the least threatening. A widow of less than considerable means, she dared not risk losing her home, compromising her son's career, or alienating those supporters of the Abbey whose commitment was to cultural rather than to political nationalism. Yeats wished Abbey policy to remain apolitical, and Miss Horniman, whom Lady Gregory categorized as "mad to boot," was outraged at the faintest wisp of political smoke. It is not coincidental that when Horniman withdrew her support because the Abbey failed to shut down in mourning for Edward VII, Lady Gregory produced, almost immediately, a play which Malcolm Brown calls "the most daring addition to literary Parnellism since O'Grady's."[5]

In several interviews to the New York press during the winter 1911–12 tour of the Abbey, Lady Gregory traced the inspiration for the Irish dramatic movement to "the moment after Parnell's death" when "his party broke up" and "the imagination of Irishmen . . . looked about for something to pitch on."[6] For many Irish writers, as Herbert Howarth demonstrates, the imagination may have been set free, but it frequently pitched on the source of its liberation. It was the fateful coincidence of the tragic events of Parnell's decline and the archetypes in Irish history and myth that it actualized that stimulated much creativity. Remote historical fact and mythological tradition reappeared in the pattern of Parnell's rise, fall and, some would add, resurrection. Lady Gregory was among the first to observe this phenomenon: myth was becoming history, and history, myth. The Parnell of whom she writes, however, does not, like Robinson's "Lost Leader," leap full-bodied out of the grave.[7] Rather, she creates a Parnell who is an active ghost of another kind whose subtle presence enriches the texture and resonance of many of her plays, most especially *The Deliverer, Dervorgilla*, and her most fatalistic tragedy, *Grania*.

Parnell's presence is most obvious in the tragic-comedy, *The Deliverer*, first performed at the Abbey on 12 January 1911—less than two months after Miss Horniman's hasty exit. The association between Parnell and Moses, on which the play depends, did not, of course, begin with Lady Gregory. Ironically, it was first made by Gladstone in October 1881, before Parnell was sentenced to Kilmainham for his opposition to the Land Act.[8] It was an association which Parnell himself was not reluctant to exploit,[9] and it was one which John F. Taylor's rhetoric in the "Aeolus" chapter of *Ulysses* assures us was a Dublin commonplace in 1904. Elizabeth Coxhead's objection that Lady Gregory's Moses has "little resemblance to either Moses or Parnell"[10] fails to appreciate the ease with which the association was made and the skill with which Lady Gregory's rewriting of scripture brings the Moses/Parnell correspondences into clear focus. Both share physical charm, Romantic appeal, and a capacity for calculating judgment and social aloofness that is mistaken for demonic pride. Like Parnell, Lady Gregory's Moses has adopted the mannerisms and speech of the "King of Foreign" with whom he lives. He is hardly distinguishable from the members of the "over-government," and the mob is amazed to discover that he is "of our own race and of our tribe."[11] Moreover, the title "uncrowned king" is exploited in Lady Gregory's calling her Moses "the King's heir" and describing him as one who "is apt to be made king in the finish." A reference to the O'Shea affair appears when Ard, who eventually betrays Moses, suggests that "There is talk of a young queen is looking out from her window for him" (*Deliverer* 258). This is perhaps intended to evoke the notorious image of Parnell's use of the fire escape in his visits to Mrs. O'Shea—an image used with understandable delight by his detractors.

The association of Parnell with Moses includes, of course, an association of the Irish in bondage to the English with the Jews in bondage to the Egyptians—an association used also by Joyce, Moore, and Yeats. Like the Jews of the Old Testament, the Irish of *The Deliverer* long for some revelation as a means to achieve freedom and take their courage from an heroic past. But the strength of Lady Gregory's play rests not in revealing the historic coincidence but in attending to the tragic distinction: the historical Jews achieved their freedom, and the Irish, as we find them handcuffed at the end of the play, do not. The incongruities to which Coxhead objects are the source of the play's irony and are among its most persuasive strengths. To assist her nationalist purpose, Lady Gregory rewrites scripture so that the Irish are revealed as self-afflicting agents of their own destruction. They allow internal rivalry, jealousy, and religious prejudice to turn them against the one source of their hope. They do not simply revolt against Moses, as do the ancient Jews; they actually kill him, throw him to the king's cats who "claw you . . . bite you, and put poison in your veins the same as a serpent, as maybe they might be in the early time of the world" (*Deliverer* 258–59).

Lady Gregory's man-eating cats parody Parnell's infamous wolves, howling for his destruction. She, however, extends the significance of her cats far beyond Parnell's wolves by associating the English not only with destructive beasts but also with Satan, original sin, and the very origins of primal evil. It is clear, too, that she wished to evoke the association anti-Parnellites made between Mrs. O'Shea and "cats" when they reduced her Christian name to its diminutive, "Kitty." In addition, she suggests that the betrayal of Parnell/Moses was grounded in no real moral issue but in the pettiness of the

Irish nation. Dan and Ard, who at first support Moses, become consumed with sexual jealousy when their wives are seduced by Moses' romantic charms. To break his spell, they discredit Moses not in authentic political language but in contrived moral and religious terms. This assessment of the motivation behind Parnell's downfall was shared by Parnellite forces, among whom were many of Lady Gregory's friends. In her *Autobiography,* she reports her visits to A. W. Kinglake who during the O'Shea v. Parnell trial "liked to see me every day that I might tell him what was going on and 'clear his mind.' When he heard of the repudiation of Parnell by the Liberals on moral grounds, 'Hypocrites,' he said vehemently from beneath his covering, with the old energy and fire."[12] Also, she does not fail to include mention of the responsibility of the clergy in contributing to Parnell's ruin. Ard meets one of the Egyptian priests who dissuades him from rebellion in language which echoes that common among the Irish clergy. "Go quiet and easy," the priest says, "the King would be apt to come around, and let us go free in the heel (*Deliverer* 271). In 1890, Archbishop Croke of Cashel wrote to Justin McCarthy, pressing on him the need that Parnell ease out of the political scene "quietly and with good grace."[13] Similarly, Archbishop Walsh of Dublin advised, "Take time. There never was a cause more clearly requiring calm and full deliberation."[14] Ard indeed breaks Moses' spell, and the mob who loved him because he was "as nice as you'd ask" now throw him to the cats so "no one will recognize him. They'll have the face ate off him ere morning" (*Deliverer* 276).

Lady Gregory defines the "tragic" in terms that recall Yeats:

> . . . tragedy shows humanity in the grip of circumstances, of fate, of what our people call "the thing will happen," "the Woman in the Stars that does all." . . . Well, you put your actor in the grip of this woman, in the claws of the cat. Once in that grip you know what the end must be. You may let your hero kick or struggle, but he is in the claws all

the time, it is a mere question as to how nearly you will let him escape, and when you will allow the pounce. Fate itself is the protagonist, your actor cannot carry much character, it is out of place. You do not want to know the character of a wrestler you see trying his strength at a show.[15]

In *The Deliverer,* Moses/Parnell is literally tossed into the claws of a devouring cat, and Malachi's fatalistic view of history seems to confirm that Irish freedom is unattainable. But the Moses of Lady Gregory's play and the Parnell of popular myth transcend ordinary limits and return from the dead. After the cats have destroyed him and the Jews break into internal debate, the figure of Moses arises:

Dan's Wife: Look! He is living yet. He is passing!
Dan: It is but his ghost. He is vanished from us. . . . Will he never come back to us?
Malachi: . . . no man will see the body is put in the grave. A strange thing to get the goal, and the lad of the goal being dead. . . . I wouldn't wonder at all he to bring back cross money to shoot the cats. He will get satisfaction on the cats.
[*Deliverer* 277]

Malachi's speech recalls Parnell's request of 2 December 1890: "If I am to leave you tonight, I should like to leave you in security. I should like—and it is not an unfair thing for me to ask—that I should come within sight of the promised land."[16] It is a prophecy, not unlike that made by his Old Testament prototype, which is neither fatalistic nor tragic but is rather confident in the success of a Messiah who will elude the grip of cyclic time, the residual effects of evil, and the lengthy bondage to the King of Foreign. Like the verse scrawled across the back of Parnell's photograph, it predicts the victory of a man who has died. If the tragic elements in the play rest in the distance between Jewish success and Irish failure, the comic elements emerge when the figure Moses/ Parnell becomes Christ/Parnell and the hope of deliverance, placed in the mouth of the prophet Malachi, arises not from disputes about past guilts but in response to future responsibilities.

Dervorgilla opened at the Abbey on 31 October 1907, only nine months after the *Playboy* riots. In 1891 anti-Parnellite forces had run through Irish villages brandishing women's undergarments as flags of protest against the adultery of Mrs. O'Shea and Parnell. In 1907, the association of Irish peasant womanhood with "shifts" in Synge's play was more than the unforgiving Dublin audience could tolerate. Yeats's speech to the audience a few days after the riots was addressed primarily to the young, both those who engaged in such personal attacks and those more praiseworthy Irish youths who, "weary of the tyranny of clubs and leagues," see that the root of manhood is "courage and honesty." Lady Gregory's *Dervorgilla* may be her response to the same rioting crowd. It is certainly her own meditation on the "swift, terrible judgment of the young."

Although, unlike *The Deliverer*, *Dervorgilla* is not a straightforward allegory in which the correspondences between a received tradition and contemporary political events can be so clearly drawn, it nonetheless suggests that Lady Gregory saw in the adultery of Dervorgilla and Diarmuid a type of the adulterous relationship of Katharine O'Shea and Parnell. She exploits the correspondence to strengthen the fabric of her play and to increase its didactic effect. In her *Autobiography*, Lady Gregory mentions Mrs. O'Shea only once, and it is interesting, in light of the focus that *Dervorgilla* takes, to note what aspect of Mrs. O'Shea's character she chooses to remember:

> 1 March, 1897: At dinner with the Grant Duffs. Sir Wilfred Lawson was enthusiastic about the *Life of Parnell*, so I asked him to meet Barry O'Brien and Yeats one evening at dinner, and he came and we had a very pleasant talk. B. O'B. told us that Lewis told him he had gone to

Brighton to take Parnell's directions about the case, and Mrs. O'Shea came in and interrupted and gave her opinion. Lewis said, "I was employed by Mr. Parnell," but she said, "he will do as I wish," and Parnell sat there meek and mild.[17]

In her account of Dervorgilla in the *Kiltartan History*, she emphasizes especially that Dervorgilla "was not brought away by force, she went to MacMurrough herself."[18] In both relationships it is the wilfulness of the female and the reticence of the male that point out the responsible partner.

One of Lady Gregory's sources for *Dervorgilla* was Giraldus Cambrensis, whose history of Ireland begins with "for as Mark Anthony and Troy are witnesses, almost all the greatest evils in the world have arisen from women." It is his description of Diarmuid, however, that most attracted Lady Gregory:

> Dermitius was tall in stature, and of large proportions, and being a great warrior and valiant in his nation, his voice had become hoarse by constantly shouting and raising his war-cry in battle. Bent more on inspiring fear than love, he oppressed his nobles, though he advanced the lowly.[19]

As she rewrote scripture in *The Deliverer*, she rewrites history in *Dervorgilla* to emphasize those aspects of it most useful to her nationalist ends. She places this description of Diarmuid in the mouth of Dervorgilla:

> He had liefer be dreaded than loved! It was he cast down the great, it was the dumb poor he served! Every proud man against him and he against every proud man. Oh, Diarmuid, I did not dread you. It was I myself led you astray!
>
> [*Dervorgilla* 108]

The Diarmuid of the play is, of course, a far more noble character than that drawn by Giraldus. He is designed to evoke sympathy: he takes advantage of popular descriptions of Parnell as cold and aloof and places the blame for his fall entirely on the determinations of a seductive woman.

Dervorgilla is about the remorse of her whose adultery first brought the English into Ireland. Although it is impossible to equate Dervorgilla with the widowed Mrs. Parnell, it would be clear to a staunch Parnellite that, if Katharine O'Shea was not herself responsible for bringing the English into Ireland, she certainly caused their prolonged stay.[20] The play presents the spectacle of a woman whose guilt, however, we are asked to forgive. The lesson the play teaches is that the failure to forgive the past encourages tragedy in the present. In the *Kiltartan History*, the idealized peasants forgive both Dervorgilla and Diarmuid: he because he had a "coaxing way" and she because "sometimes women are weak." They are also able to forgive Parnell and Mrs. O'Shea: "How do we know but that was a thing appointed for him by God?"[21] But the youths of *Dervorgilla* who assemble at Mellifont to receive their trophies are not. Like the youths addressed by Yeats, they are members of a club, a sports league, and are still the victims of its tyranny. It is, ironically, a misguided poet who leads them further astray. Without ideals or wisdom and driven by poverty, the poet stirs up bitter memories of the past and encourages the youths to reproach Dervorgilla rather than forgive her. They turn to the English who "look to be friendly enough," with the result that another Irishman is killed. The cycle of history is repeated because the Irish youth cannot forgive.

The play, like so many other of Lady Gregory's plays, raises far more questions than it answers. She no doubt intended it as one of those plays on history that schools and colleges might incorporate as part of a day's lesson. Certainly the significance of her questions broadens if the association between twelfth century history and contemporary events is made. Dervorgilla asks, "Can a wrong once done ever be undone?"; "Could that person ever gain forgiveness, praying and sorrowing?"; "But if that neighbour, that stranger, that race, should turn kind and honest, or could be sent back, and all be as before, would not forgiveness be gained by that?" (*Dervorgilla* 100).

Lady Gregory examines the full effects of the failure to forgive in *Grania*. Here she rewrites not scripture or history but Irish myth. One of the mysteries that surrounds the play arises from Lady Gregory's refusal to allow it to be performed during her lifetime. Written in 1911 and called her most ambitious attempt to dramatize myth,[22] it has remained unproduced. Her own comments about the play invite speculation:

> I think I turned to Grania because so many have written about sad, lovely Deirdre, who when overtaken by sorrow made no good battle at the last. Grania had more power of will, and for good or evil twice took the shaping of her life into her own hands. The riddle she asks us through the ages is, "Why did I, having left great, grey-haired Finn for comely Diarmuid, turn back to Finn in the end, when he had consented to Diarmuid's death"? And a question tempts one more than the beaten path of authorised history.[23]

Grania aims to provide one answer to this riddle, but it is one, when read in the light of contemporary history, that is pessimistic enough to dissuade Lady Gregory from allowing its production. So black are its conclusions that its production could do little to fire the nationalist cause.

Lady Gregory's accommodations of her own account of the myth of Diarmuid and Grania in *Gods and Fighting Men* reveal a part of her intention in writing the play. The most obvious of these accommodations is the reduction of characters to three, a reduction on which she was most insistent even in the face of Yeats's criticism. While it is true that the play removes the heroic background from which the characters spring—an accommodation, by the way, which allows us to appreciate the contemporaneity of their situation, they emerge, nonetheless, as fully realized human beings whose motivations are capable of psychological investigation. For example, in *Gods and Fighting Men*, the relationship between

Diarmuid and Finn is merely a feudal one, while in *Grania*, Diarmuid is Finn's "son," servant and friend. Finn cannot forgive Diarmuid because he "reared on his knee and nourished with every marrow-bone" (*Grania* 32) the man who eventually betrays him. Also, in the legend Diarmuid and Finn are not so sharply contrasted to one another as they are in the play. While the Finn in the legend is grey-haired and old, there is no indication that his prowess as a lover has been weakened. Diarmuid says to Grania, "It is a wonder you give that love to me, and not to Finn . . . for there is not in Ireland a man is a better lover to a woman than himself." In *Grania*, however, Finn is very much in physical and spiritual decline and despairs over Diarmuid's vitality and youth. He is not surrounded by troops and useful, if sometimes disloyal, advisors, but rather his betrayal by Diarmuid is far more intense because it had been on him alone that Finn was able to rely. Moreover, the legend in no way suggests that the willful seduction by a woman separates a dying man from the personal embodiments of his own hopes. The three-character play frees the legend from all but its most essential details and, like *Dervorgilla*, presents a tragedy of triangular love in which a willful, seductive and adulterous woman is the agent of personal and political discord.

Hazard Adams's description of the dramatic Grania as "a more naïve and conventionally romantic heroine" than the legendary Grania is unjustified.[24] If anything, the situation is reversed. The play presents her as an epicurean opportunist who from the very beginning instigates evil, sees its immediate effects, and yet persists in her determination. Moreover, since the play does not allow us to share in Grania's years of hardship with Diarmuid, we are not moved by her suffering. We see her continually prodding, urging Diarmuid to leave the woods and seek the society of men where he will be captured and destroyed. She persuades him not to make peace with Finn, and it is only in Act III that we get some sense of the actual depth of her love. Here, however, that love quickly turns to revenge. Grania, like Dervorgilla, assumes responsibility for all the evil that she causes, and we are given no reason to argue with her. If there is a romantic figure in the play, it is Diarmuid whose very downfall is rooted in an act of chivalry. Finn describes him as one who "would find it hard to do anything was not mannerly, and befitting a man reared in king's houses." Unlike the Diarmuid of *Gods and Fighting Men*, he makes his original breach with Finn in a defense of Grania, and it is Diarmuid who, much to Grania's chagrin, proposes chastity as an ideal. It is finally Diarmuid's sense of chivalry that Finn uses to trick him into fighting the King of Foreign. As Ellis-Fermor observes, the Diarmuid of the play is not so much a man of real, definable passion as he is a "Tennysonian knight-errant"[25]—an ideal hero, above reproach and not unlike Moses of *The Deliverer*.

In addition to giving more specific shape to her characters, Lady Gregory also made significant alterations in plot detail. The duration of Diarmuid's wanderings are shortened to seven years. The omission of Angus Og and Finn's nurse eliminates all supernatural elements, and forces attention to free choice and responsibility. Still retained in the play are the loaf of bread as a token of fidelity, the almost accidental breaking of the oath, Finn's final revenge through trickery, and the jeering of the mob when Grania finally appears as Finn's new bride. However, in attempting to understand the question of Grania's return to Finn—an event limited to one line in the legend—the play's final act is taken up almost entirely with Finn's renewed suit of Grania, his decision to desist, and return to Almhuid. In the play, the decision to return to Finn belongs to Grania alone.

Written only a few months after *The Deliverer*, *Grania* concludes with a similar resurrection from the dead. It might be argued that in the case of *Grania*, Diarmuid's death is only apparent. But it seems that in Finn's concluding his examination of Diarmuid's wound with "he is dead indeed," we may read at least the suggestion that Diarmuid's final words about mutual forgiveness come from beyond the grave. But while Moses' eventual "satisfaction on the cats" transmutes tragedy into comedy, the tragedy of *Grania* is unrelieved.

In his last speech, Diarmuid repudiates his alliance with Grania: "It would be a very foolish thing, any woman at all to have leave to come between yourself and myself" (*Grania* 42). Lady Gregory's answer to the riddle of Grania's return is Grania's need for revenge. She will not allow the sacrifice of her life for Diarmuid to go unnoticed. She, not Diarmuid, will get satisfaction, and that satisfaction will consist in her preventing the breach between Diarmuid and Finn from ever healing. The prediction made by the old people at the start of the play, that there is no good news in love at all, has come true. The movement of the play is circular and downward. The queen's crown, the golden dress, the gathering crowd of Act I are all there again in Act III to underscore the absurdity of all the suffering that has gone between. Finn is now older and more hopeless; Grania is mocked rather than cheered; Finn finally predicts, "There will be no more joy in anything happens from this day out forever" (*Grania* 43).

Such unremitting fatalism is absent from the legend as it is from the other plays. The capacity for forgiveness that Finn manifests in *Grania* is that which the children in *Dervorgilla* disdain, yet it is only a fatuous gesture in the face of remorseless circumstance. The futility expressed in *Grania* is inconsistent with the ideals of the nationalist movement as Lady Gregory envisioned them, and it is an expression of deep personal despair. To stage it would be counter-productive to her single-minded nationalist commitment.[26]

The accommodations of character and plot suggest that Lady Gregory's adaptation of her own account of the legend as a work for the stage encourages a reading of the play as another statement about Parnell. In Finn we may see the decline of Ireland's heroic ideal; in Diarmuid, the embodiment of the future vitality of that ideal as it was focused in Parnell; and in Grania, the adulterous woman whose presence haunted turn-of-the-century Irish politics and splintered the nationalist movement. The re-creation of Diarmuid as a thoroughly romantic hero is consistent with the image of Parnell presented by the popular Parnellite press, with the image that Lady Gregory exploits in *The Deliverer,* and with the veiled image of him that Yeats defended in Norreys Connell's *The Piper.*[27] Grania imagines the women of Ireland jealous of her success with Diarmuid, and in emphasizing Diarmuid's chivalry, Lady Gregory was perhaps inspired by Parnell's defense of Mrs. O'Shea against the attack of Tim Healy. Parnell called Healy a "cowardly little scoundrel . . . that . . . dares to insult a woman,"[28] and although it clearly strains credibility to suggest that Healy is the inspiration for Finn, the intense feeling of personal betrayal that emerges from his late exchanges with Parnell is similar to those of the play.

The addition of Diarmuid's resurrection to the play is grounded in the popular belief that either Parnell had not been buried in Glasnevin at all, or if he had, his ghost was still at large appearing to selected followers in Ireland and abroad—not the least significant being between the acts of *Siegfried* in far-away Bayreuth.[29] Lady Gregory kept both Tynan's lament and the scrap of old ballad copied on the back of Parnell's photo. In her play, Diarmuid appears to Grania not simply in the flesh and blood told about in the legend but also "sometimes he came through my dreams"—language parallel to that of the old and treasured ballad. Moreover, although the play does not show us Diarmuid torn apart by wolves or cats, Grania first sees him fighting off a pack of wild dogs, "hounds the strange men had brought with them" (*Grania* 15). Similarly, in the legend Diarmuid is tricked into fighting a wild boar, while in the play, Finn sends him off to fight "the King of Foreign"—an epithet which appears nowhere in *Gods and Fighting Men* but quite frequently in *The Deliverer*.

The unsympathetic portrait of Grania in the play is similar to that drawn of Mrs. O'Shea in *Vanity Fair* (22 November 1890) when it named her the "were-wolf woman of Irish politics"; or as Tim Healy described her in a speech in July 1891: "One bad, base, immoral woman. Parnell broke his pledge to Ireland, Kitty broke her vow to her husband . . . the person at the bottom of the whole business is Mrs. O'Shea." The play, unlike the legend, reports that hatred for Grania is widespread among the common people who call her a "low-born . . . hedgehog, an ugly thing" (*Grania* 39). Yet when

Grania emerges at the end of the play, now as a queen, the mob who at first reviles her, soon grows silent under the power of her will. The final silence is frightening and is perhaps Lady Gregory's most despairing comment on the cowering indifference of the Irish mob. As Lady Gregory tells us, Grania has more power of will than Deirdre, but it is a power for evil. In modeling her Grania on the popular image of Mrs. O'Shea, she suggests that although Ireland has lost its uncrowned king, it has gained a crowned and wicked queen whose indomitable presence haunted Irish politics for over twenty-five crucial years. It is not the cats who are avenged, but they who remain the avengers.

Had Lady Gregory produced *Grania*, she would have contributed to a popular remembrance of Parnell, not as a real and salvific historical figure, but rather as a successor of the archetypal failed hero, Diarmuid. It would have helped to bind further the already constricted collective memory into an unbreakable pattern of eternal recurrence. The nightmare of history would have deepened and her dream of a dawn would have been reduced to hopeless absurdity. The tragedy of *Grania* lies not in the will of its heroine, as Ronsley and others suggest, but in the velleity of the Irish mob. It is not a single actor who is caught in the claws of a cat, but the anonymous crowd whose memory cannot retain history's forgivable distinctions but only its damning repetitions. If Lady Gregory's play tells the truth, then the real Parnell becomes what Mircea Eliade would call "a falsification."[30] The play becomes truer than history because it makes history yield a dark significance which reveals for Ireland a thoroughly tragic destiny. Such was not the intention of Lady Gregory's rebel nationalism.

When Finn describes his feelings on the night of his betrayal, he says to Grania, "For my life was as if cut in two halves on that night that put me to and fro; and the half that was full and flowing was put behind me, and it has been all on the ebb since then" (*Grania* 38). It is not only the collapse of the Fianna, the disintegration of Ireland's band of heroic giants, that may be traced to the coming of the Lochlannachs—those little but crafty men "who used to be humbugging them." In Finn's speech we may also read Lady Gregory's evaluation of the split in Irish politics that followed Parnell's fall and the triumph of pettiness, indifference, and intolerance of the majority of her Irish contemporaries. At least two years before September 1913, Lady Gregory saw that Romantic Ireland was dead and gone. The full intention of Finn's speech becomes clearer as he continues:

> . . . it is a king is lost from them this day. And if you have no mind to keen him, let you raise a keen for the men of your own country he left dumb in the dust, and a foolish smile on their face. For he was a good man to put down his enemies and the enemies of Ireland, and it is living he would be this day if it was not for his great comeliness and the way he had that sent every woman stammering after him and coveting him; and it was love of a woman brought him down in the end, and sent him astray in the world. [*Grania* 43]

In March 1919, Lady Gregory stepped onto the stage of the Abbey as Cathleen ni Houlihan. She is said to have rivaled Sara Allgood and to have overcome the physical handicap of her small and dumpy stature: one saw only "the fine carriage of her head and her noble brow." It was perhaps the first time she could so publicly express the spirit that so quietly inhabits so many of her plays. If as Cathleen ni Houlihan, she could confidently promise the youth of Ireland that should they die for her tomorrow, they would be remembered and live forever, it is because as Lady Gregory she had so singlemindedly committed herself to winning a fight a dead man had long ago lost. In both temperament, vision, and calling, she resembled her hero, Parnell. If, as she tells us in *Gods and Fighting Men*, the redemption of Ireland lay in its stories, Parnell's story must be among those frequently told. By repeating his story and the similar stories of his heroic predecessors, Ireland will win back, she tells us, the hearts it has lost and "will begin again to be a Holy Land."

NOTES

1. Ann Saddlemyer, "Augusta Gregory, Irish Nationalist: 'After All, What is Wanted but a Hag and a Voice,'" in *Myth and Reality in Irish Literature*, ed. Joseph Ronsley (Waterloo, Ontario, Canada: Wilfred Laurier University Press, 1977), p. 29. This essay is by far the most persuasive and concise defense of Lady Gregory's nationalism, and traces its general development from her early work with Yeats and Douglas Hyde until her death.

2. Quoted in Hazard Adams, *Lady Gregory* (Lewisburg: Bucknell University Press, 1973), pp. 39–40.

3. Isabella Augusta Gregory, *Lady Gregory's Journals, 1916–1930*, ed. Lennox Robinson (New York: Macmillan, 1947); Isabella Augusta Gregory, *Seventy Years, Being the Autobiography of Lady Gregory*, ed. Colin Smythe (New York: Macmillan, 1974); Isabella Augusta Gregory, *Lady Gregory's Journals, Volume One*, ed. Daniel J. Murphy (New York: Oxford University Press, 1978).

4. Quoted in Robinson, "Editor's Foreword," *Lady Gregory's Journals, 1916–1930*, p. 8.

5. Malcolm Brown, *The Politics of Irish Literature: From Thomas Davis to W. B. Yeats* (Seattle, Wash.: University of Washington Press, 1972), p. 378.

6. "How Ireland Turned from Politics to Playwriting," *The New York Times Magazine* (3 December 1911), p. 5; reprinted in *Lady Gregory: Interviews and Recollections*, ed. E. H. Mikhail (Totowa, N.J.: Rowman and Littlefield, 1977), p. 56.

7. Lennox Robinson's *The Lost Leader* (Belfast: H. R. Carter, 1954) was first produced at the Abbey on 19 February 1918. Lady Gregory comments in her *Journals* that on 14 April 1920, she listened to a run through of the play, and suggested that Robinson change its ending by giving Parnell this final speech: "I have learned that my generation has passed. I have no more to do I will leave it to the lads in Mountjoy" (Murphy, *Lady Gregory's Journals, Volume One*, p. 140).

8. *Daily News*, 8 October 1881.

9. See F. S. L. Lyons, *Charles Stewart Parnell* (New York: Oxford University Press, 1977), p. 520.

10. Elizabeth Coxhead, *Lady Gregory: A Literary Portrait* (New York: Harcourt, Brace & World, 1961), p. 103.

11. Isabella Augusta Gregory, *The Deliverer*, in *The Tragic-Comedies of Lady Gregory, Being the Second Volume of the Collected Plays*, ed. Ann Saddlemyer (New York: Oxford University Press, 1970), p. 257. Subsequent citations from *The Deliverer* and from Lady Gregory's *Dervorgilla* and *Grania* are from this Coole Edition of the plays, and will be indicated parenthetically in the text.

12. Gregory, *Seventy Years*, p. 138.

13. Quoted in Lyons, *Charles Stewart Parnell*, p. 514.

14. Ibid., p. 513.

15. Isabella Augusta Gregory, "Notes" to *Damer's Gold*, in *New Comedies* (New York: Putnam, 1913), pp. 158–59.

16. Quoted in Lyons, *Charles Stewart Parnell*, p. 520.

17. Gregory, *Seventy Years*, p. 341.

18. Isabella Augusta Gregory, *The Kiltartan History Book* (London: T. Fisher Unwin, 1926), p. 37.

19. Giraldus Cambrensis, *The History of the Conquest of Ireland*, trans. Thomas Forester; ed. Thomas Wright (London: H. G. Bohn, 1863), pp. 196–97.

20. See James Joyce in "Notes by the Author" accompanying *Exiles:* "The two greatest Irishmen of modern times—Swift and Parnell—broke their lives over women. And it was the adulterous wife of the King of Leinster who brought the first Saxon to the Irish coast" (Harmondsworth: Penguin, 1973), p. 160.

21. Gregory, *Kiltartan History Book,* pp. 37, 95.

22. Una Ellis-Fermor, *The Irish Dramatic Movement* (London: Methuen, 1939), p. 154.

23. Gregory, "Notes and Music," in *Collected Plays,* p. 283.

24. Adams, *Lady Gregory,* p.54.

25. Ellis-Fermor, *The Irish Dramatic Movement,* p. 158.

26. See also Joseph Ronsley, "Lady Gregory's *Grania,*" *Canadian Journal of Irish Studies* 3, no. 1 (1977): 41–58. Ronsley's reading is far more traditional than that presented here, but because it insists, with Adams, that Grania is in the last analysis a sympathetic character, it still must rest on certain self-admitted contradictions which seem to leave the problems presented by the play, and Lady Gregory's comments on it, unresolved.

27. *Freeman's Journal,* 17 February 1908. Yeats sees in the character "Black Mike" an image of Parnell. Parnell may well be the inspiration for any number of other Abbey plays, among them Lennox Robinson's *Patriots* (Dublin and London: Maunsel, 1912) which begins with a dedication from Lady Gregory's *The Image,* and An Craoibhin's *The Lost Saint* which Lady Gregory includes in *Poets and Dreamers* (London: Murray, 1903). Immediately before the inclusion of the An Craoibhin plays, Lady Gregory has written, "But here, on the edge of the world, dreams are real things, and every heart is watching for the opening of one or another grave" (p. 195). See also Harold Orel, "A Drama for the Nation," *Irish History and Culture,* ed. Harold Orel (Lawrence: Kansas University Press, 1976), pp. 251–69; and Ann Saddlemyer, "Stars of the Abbey's Ascendancy," *Theater and Nationalism in Twentieth-Century Ireland,* ed. Robert O'Driscoll (Toronto: University of Toronto Press, 1971), pp. 21–39.

28. Quoted in Joyce Marlow, *The Uncrowned Queen of Ireland: The Life of "Kitty" O'Shea* (New York: Dutton, 1975), p. 256.

29. The incident is reported by John Dillon in his "Diary" 27 September 1894 and discussed by F. S. L. Lyons in "The Parnell Theme in Literature," *Place, Personality and the Irish Writer,* ed. Andrew Carpenter (New York: Barnes and Noble [Irish Literary Studies I], 1977), p. 94. See also Hans Walter Gabler, "The Christmas Dinner Scene, Parnell's Death and the Genesis of *A Portrait of the Artist as a Young Man,*" *James Joyce Quarterly* 13 (Fall 1975): 27–38.

30. Mircea Eliade, *The Myth of the Eternal Return,* 2d ed. (Princeton: Princeton University Press, 1965), pp. 45–46.

French Reporter Visits Volunteers' Training Camp,
"Somewhere" in Western Ireland, August 15, 1921

Translation of Chapter V "Guerilla Liberation" from Ireland: Eye-Witness *by Simone Téry[1]*

Translated by Marilyn Gaddis Rose

Simone Téry (1897–1967), intrepid, faintly fatale *Frenchwoman, did her investigating for* Ireland: Eye-Witness *during the six-month Truce, July-December, 1921. The "Tan War" had been halted, and the Second Dail, which began its session the day after Téry dispatched this story, was trying to settle down to govern the country and work out its side of the Treaty. Téry, who would soon form a lifelong friendship with AE, adopted his political views on Ireland and became eventually a Free State partisan. It is evident from her report of this excursion with Michael Brennan that she found this Free State stalwart immediately sympathetic. It is evident also that in mid-August, 1921, she was not even looking for hints of grievous post-Treaty turmoil. She was to know the latter well at first-hand, for* Ireland: Eye-Witness *reveals not only the evolution of mood of the Irish but also her evolution as an Irish sympathizer. Her uncritical girlish enthusiasm changes into discriminating support.*

Although she was never to cover Irish politics again, she

published a subsequent essay on an enduring form of nationalism: Isle of Bards, *a literary survey valuable for its interpolated impressions of Yeats, Joyce, James Stephens, and AE whose opinions informed hers.*[2] *However,* Ireland: Eye-Witness *established the pattern of her career. Because of it she broke with her father Gustave Téry, founding editor of* L'Oeuvre, Le Matin, *and* Le Journal. *She sought out anticapitalist trouble spots, not where fighting was full scale but where guerilla warfare allowed her to defend herself with bluff, charm, and a canny appeal to chivalry. One of the first to recognize Nazism, she threatened a hunger strike (she later said Irish patriots gave her the idea) if* Le Journal *would not print her exposé.*[3] *She went to China, was jailed in Madrid, fell under Stalin's spell, lived with Greek Partisans. In 1935 she joined the French Communist Party and its daily* L'Humanité *with which she was affiliated until her death.*

Her peripatetic life and her break with her affluent left-of-center family may explain why records of her are largely limited to her works, numerous but out of print. It is certainly the case that these are all we could draw on, although we have been trying since mid-summer 1978 to discover whether any drafts, notes, papers (or heirs) still exist. Her notes would have been more valuable than her published interviews because we can tell from the French that she was taking notes in English.

Thus, this translation has actually been an exercise in traduction-retour *("translation-back")—with the original control text lost. The reportage format has other drawbacks for translation. Téry was writing rapidly, sometimes carelessly, sometimes in journalese at its worst. Operating in a foreign language, she did not always hear names correctly. She must not always have matched answer to question correctly, nor seized exactly what was said. Sometimes* her *translations have to be wrong.*

But she was there. An outside observer, she was free to send back reports which, as we have verified, could not appear in the Establishment press. Her sympathy and sensitivity are genuine, and her flair for noting the telling detail is unfailing.

We should like to acknowledge the prompt and gracious cooperation of René Andrieu, editor in chief of L'Humanité.

General Michael Brennan.—The Irish countryside.—Ruins of war and poverty.—Popular enthusiasm.—How the Volunteers train.—Guerilla warfare.—A man, once condemned, remembers.—The leader adored.—Police at the door.—Soldiers.—The village dance.

How could Ireland, poor and unarmed, hold out so long against the Empire and its formidable arsenal? And if the Truce is broken, will the Irish be able to keep up their resistance?

"It's best if you size it up for yourself," they told me at government headquarters. "Tomorrow, Michael Brennan, Commandant in Chief for County Clare, is going back to the West. You will go with him. . . ."

* * *

In the Irish Republican Army, there are only two grades, captain and commandant. Each man carries out the duties of his rank (which only the members know) without worrying about stripes and titles. As a result, when a Volunteer is captured, it is hard to know whether he's a superior officer. But everyone knows that Michael Brennan—along with "Murderer" [Eoin] MacKeon probably the most popular of the Volunteers—is Commandant in Chief. (This corresponds to a French divisional general [U.S. major general].) I don't know anything about Mihall Brennan's military qualifications (his English name Michael is given Gaelic pronunciation, and most people call him by his first name), but he looks like a young war god. Whenever he goes down the street, heads turn to admire his vigorous physique, broad shoulders, and perfectly beautiful head. His curly hair is so thick that he is bothered by his battle helmet. His forehead is high, and his eyebrows heavy. His large, deep eyes seem to survey the horizon. His mouth is serious, a little pinched; his nose and chin are regular and forceful. When you look at this twenty-

French Reporter Visits Volunteers' Training Camp

five-year-old general, you remember the martial beauty of our young Revolutionary generals like Hoch and Marceau.

* * *

"Well, General, can you rest during the Truce?"

"What do you mean, rest? We've never had so much to do. And this isn't so much fun as our other work."

"But what are you doing?"

"You'll see all that tomorrow, when we're at my general headquarters. Today, as we drive along, you are going to see the effects of war, and that will help you understand how we prepare our defense."

The automobile was leaving the dark Dublin suburbs.

"What's that large barracks, darker than the other buildings?"

"That's the South Dublin Workhouse."

A workhouse? All Dickens came back to me. All his eloquence and indignation against these asylums, more sinister than prisons.

"And what is that building over there? It doesn't look too cheerful either."

"That's Kilmainham Jail where the Insurgents of 1916 faced the firing squad."

The General's voice got heavier. His eyes clouded over.

"And that building which is like a fortress, is it a prison, too?"

"No, but it amounts to the same thing. That's the Richmond Barracks where they were condemned to death."

And still another building, more imposing than the others, and more forbidding.

"That's Maryborough Prison, the fashionable prison where distinguished prisoners—all the leaders—are interned. But they're no better treated there."

"Am I to believe that in your country there are only prisons and workhouses?"

"Exactly. That's the English government for you. It's quite simple. When they don't put us in the workhouse, they put us in prison, and when they don't put us in prison, they put us in the workhouse. To make the whole thing work, you need a lot of soldiers. We're just now reaching their camp at Curragh, the most important in Ireland. That takes money. And who pays for it? We do."

But now we've reached the real country. And one can understand the Irishman's passionate love of his land, which he calls by women's names and sings to like a sweetheart. The Irish countryside has both the graceful charm of Normandy and the rugged character of Brittany: fields, soft as tended lawns, where cattle graze; trees everywhere—poplar, elm, ash; walls of loosely piled stones or blackberry and thorn hedges overhanging the road. From time to time, the more austere landscape of peat bogs, piles of peat cut in black cubes; reeds and ferns around glistening pools. . . . Always some misty violet hill on the horizon. The entire picture enveloped with an imperceptible haze gilded with sunshine. It's a Corot painting where you expect to see fragile forms come out to dance on the flowering grass. . . .

But what sinister sights are these—in spots that seem meant for peace and poetry? We were crossing villages that are clumps of pitiful little cottages. A door and two windows on the road. That's all, sometimes a flowerpot. Thin women, wrapped in long black shawls. Ragged, barefoot children, scampering everywhere. Houses burned down in every village. During the last war [World War I], we French had entire cities destroyed, provinces where death had struck. But behind the lines, there were cities left intact where one felt safe. Here war is everywhere, at every turn. It doesn't attack indiscriminately. It concentrates its fury on the humble. There is truly no sadder sight than these cottages in ruins, rising in the midst of a village like an example and a threat. They seem to be asking for mercy on their poor charred walls.

"But look," I pointed out, "they do as much damage to the rich. There's a big house burned down."

"No, that was *our* work. See the Republican flag flying up there, the green, orange, and white tricolor? That used to be the police station. We've cleared almost all of those vermin out of the little villages, and they've had to take shelter in the centers. . . ."

But there weren't only recent ruins, there were ruins of former times, as well. We went through villages that were half-deserted. Only a few homes still inhabited. I had never seen that.

"That's what their government has done. They impoverished our country so much in the course of time that the inhabitants either died from privation or emigrated *en masse*. Ireland, which has one of the highest birth rates in Europe, still is the only country which in living memory has seen its population cut in half."

It was not easy driving there—still more work of the Volunteers, and so thoroughly done that it couldn't be put back in order during the Truce. Roads blocked and cut everywhere, sometimes for 100-meter stretches. There are trenches, bridges caved in where you suddenly see the water shining up through a big crack. Enormous tree trunks, boulders, or broken glass are placed on the road. It must be dangerous at night. We broke down six times. We had to make detours. We got lost.

"Wait a minute," said Mihall, "I'm going to take off my dust coat. That will be our best safe-conduct."

Then he appeared in his moss-green Volunteers uniform. After that, the entire population was our guide.

"Stop! Don't go that way. The road is impassable. Take this back road."

In the villages, when the car would slow down, everyone ran after it. The boys jumped on the running board, clung to the hood, and all answered our questions at once.

"Now we're in Killaloe," the General said. "I'm in my own county now, and we won't get lost. . . . And I'll have some special stories for you. Right over there, for example, four men were shot without a hearing. . . ."

And along the rest of the way, the General pointed out ruined cottages, each with its tragedy.

"See there, on the threshold of that door they fired on a pregnant woman who was coming out quietly with a child in her arms and killed her."

"Why did they do that?"

"No reason. Pure cruelty, to terrorize the population. . . .

Over there, they fired through a window and killed the seventeen-year-old boy reading on the sill. See, there's still the hole the projectile made in the window.... Now here's a better souvenir. We surprised some Black and Tans drinking in that pub."

"You shot them while they were drinking?"

"Of course, it was more polite than shooting them thirsty.... Besides, they had time to defend themselves. They broke my arm that day, and it was set so badly that it will never be right again."

But now we were near Limerick. At a crossroads there was some fresh wreckage.

"That is my house. During the night, they chased out my mother and sister in their thin nightgowns with blows of rifle butts and made them watch the burning."

"Where are they now?"

"With friends."

"You must want to see them again...."

"Naturally, but I never have the time. Besides what's the use of seeing your own sister? You can do better with somebody else's.... There's where they burned a man alive. And he wasn't even a Republican!"

"That must have made him see the light."

"Right. He should be an excellent Sinn-Feiner in heaven.... Let's go down there. We're going to find another burned-out home at the end of the path. I know the family."

A little barefoot girl ran up with cries of delight, followed by her mother and grandmother. The son was accused of being a Volunteer, so the police had tortured the three women for information. And then one night, their home was burned down. Now they lived in a corner of the ruins under a lean-to. Some boards, some tin cans. That was all they had for furniture. But on the charred wall, what were those magnificent shining gold frames? Portraits of Pearse, Connolly, and MacDonagh, executed in 1916; they died for Ireland....

By now we were in Limerick.

"Look, you can see some Black and Tans! You've probably

never seen them. Right now, besides, they're staying in their barracks."

"But I thought they wore black and tan. I don't see any tan on their uniform."

"Yes, they've changed. They've gotten blacker."

But the General was lighthearted now. He looked happy-go-lucky. He imitated a Dublin accent for the fun of it. With his comrades, he began singing old popular songs as night fell. Then, suddenly, all together, they shouted their war cries. All was forgotten—arson, war, Auxiliaries, the dangers of tomorrow. They acted like a bunch of boys back from a Sunday outing with only the problems of youth. And whenever we passed a group, I cried out with all my might just to see what would happen, "Up De Valera! *Vive* de Valera!"

And each time "Up De Valera! Up the Republic!" surrounded and followed the car.

* * *

"Is this your general headquarters?"

"If you can call it that," laughed Mihall Brennan.

We were entering a tiny village end at X___[3] On the right-hand side there was a room so small that the table filled it completely. On the table there were maps, papers, and a portable typewriter small enough to be a toy. There were artificial flowers on the mantelpiece. Through the window came the noise and freshness of a waterfall.

"Here's where I work," the General explained.

"But where's the camp?"

"There's no more camp than there is a general headquarters. This isn't like most wars. In an ordinary war, there are two armies facing each other. Only one part of the country is occupied. Here the whole country is occupied. So we don't fight against a massed army, striking straight ahead, but against a dispersed army and striking everywhere at the same time. If we had a 'camp,' a lot of men in a single place, we'd be encircled and captured."

"Guerilla warfare?"

"Yes, but guerilla warfare is usually carried on by civilians, free-shooters, acting on their own initiative, hoping to help the regular army as they can. Here, on the contrary, we have made guerilla warfare, hit-and-miss *par excellence*, into a group enterprise. We have organized it methodically."

"How do you recruit your troops?"

"All our soldiers are volunteers. There are two kinds of Volunteers. One group keeps their civilian occupation and continues to work. They come for training in the evening or during the weekend. When they're needed, they're sent orders to rejoin their company. And then there are Volunteers in active service who form our Flying Columns. They're always in action and make war fulltime. They never sleep two nights in a row under the same roof (I don't say 'in the same bed' for they rarely have one). They're hard to catch. They know that if they're captured, they'll either be shot on the spot with a dozen bullets or, worse, tortured. . . ."

"Do you have many applicants for the job?"

"More than you can count! It's hard to know the exact figure, but we certainly have from 130 to 200 thousand soldiers. And never have Volunteers been more voluntary. They must pay for their equipment, pay for their guns, pay for each bullet they shoot (from six to 12 pence according to the caliber), even pay a subscription for their rations. . . ."

"Still, not all your soldiers have a private income. Do you send away the men who can't pay?"

"Of course not, we give them arms from the subscriptions of those who can. Because we spend next to nothing for the maintenance of the Volunteers. They are lodged and fed wherever they go, and never go lacking, I assure you. Furthermore, even though we are very poor, we still have funds for the war. Our loan drives have always succeeded."

"Once the Volunteers have signed up, what do you do with them?"

"We teach them our kind of war. But we can't drill on public parade grounds. We have to take all kinds of precautions. We train in the mountains, in isolated spots. During the Truce, fortunately, we are left alone more, and we are taking advantage of it. You will not see 'Camp X___,' but you will see the 70 officers I am training at this moment. Each officer will return to his post and back there will teach his men what he has just learned."

"What's that large building which has only a few blackened walls standing?"

"That's a barracks where we dislodged them. . . ."

"But you don't have any artillery, do you? How do you manage to take posts packed with men and machine guns?"

"It's not easy, but we take them by surprise. Someone climbs up on the roof during the night and pours on several liters of petrol and sets fire to it . . . ."

"But that's very dangerous!"

"Of course. However, we always have too many volunteers for assignments calling for cunning and risk. Besides, we have more than one trick up our sleeve. We're always looking for new ones."

So you see, this is the kind of war that suits the Irish imagination. At least, they're spared the boredom of the trenches. It's as exciting as a hunt, and success goes not only to the bravest, but to the slyest.

Behind the wrecked barracks, in the very enclosure where the Black and Tans used to do close-order drill, twenty young Republic Volunteers were exercising. They wore boots, a leather belt, a khaki shirt and tie. Most of them had the moss-green uniform. A few, however, had only dark sport clothes. And on this unmarked terrain, these Volunteers, some still in civilian clothing, carried out complicated figures with the group precision of a troop on parade or a gymnastics society.

Behind them, an officer, seated, map on his knees, instructed a group. The Volunteers came forward one at a time, picked up a map from the grass and took an examination in practical geography.

Further on, up a slope, a third "class" was learning the complicated algebra of signalling. The officer would shout, "A, I, N!" and arms would raise and lower in right, acute, and obtuse angles. Five hundred meters away, 20 Volunteers executed campaign manuevers silhouetted against the sky.

To come back we took the same snorting little automobile which—by pure miracle—had made the trip from Dublin. Three hundred meters later, we had a blowout.

"I don't want to hurt your feelings. But the Republican Army has rotten motor cars."

"But you know how poor we are," the General laughed. "And yet if that were the only problem area. But poverty from top to bottom. If you saw the arms of our poor Volunteers, their rusty old pistols, their shotguns from ages past. . . . We could mount a museum show of antiques! The autos don't matter because we can't use them much. We can use them only during the Truce. If the war were on, we'd be arrested in five minutes. Besides, we couldn't go far in an automobile. You saw yesterday how we had cut all the bridges and roads."

"But don't the country folk need to get around?"

"There's always the train to transport merchandise. And then there are the little byways which they know, too small for military vehicles, but good enough for their carts. Of course, they're inconvenienced, but that's war. . . . They themselves help us block the roads!"

"How do the English defend themselves against you?"

"When they know that the Flying Columns are in an area, they try to surround us and close in the circle. Then we have to improvise something to find a break in the chain."

"You always fight in small groups?"

"Yes. We set up ambushes, stop lorries, attack isolated posts. Once the job is done, we don't wait for reinforcements. Hit and run—that's our principle. Like Napoleon's soldiers, we win battles with our legs. Naturally, this infuriates our enemy. They cannot understand how they can have as many troops as they need and the best armament, cannons, and artillery, yet we always get the upper hand. We keep snapping at them. So the English, contemptuous, enraged, accuse us of not daring to attack them head-on, of hitting them from behind, of being 'murderers.' If they want a duel, let them give us some cannons. Then they will see if, with equal arms, we are afraid. This comic spite reminds me of the Egyptians in Shaw's *Caesar and Cleopatra*. They complain that the Romans are cowards, that they never know where they are. . . . 'They simply fight and win,' they say. That's our way. We fight as we can, and we win."

* * *

In front of the little village inn, messengers were waiting with their bicycles. Others had motorcycles lined up along the road. Suddenly the large curly head of General Michael Brennan appeared in the doorway. All stiffened to attention, clicked their heels and gave the rapid Volunteers salute. But one man came forward, timid and smiling. Mihall went happily over to him, shaking his hand and holding it. You could see he'd like to hug him.

"This is Egan," he explained to me. "One of my Volunteers, you know, a good man. I hadn't seen him since he left prison."

So this was Egan, one of the two prisoners whom British civilian and military courts have been fighting over so bitterly for the past two months. These two men had been courtmartialed to be hanged as "murderers," and they owed their life and liberty to that jurisdictional dispute.

I hadn't expected to find that lucky fellow here. He had such a narrow escape. Would I learn what a condemned man thinks about?

"Cut off in my prison as I was, I didn't know these gentlemen were fighting over my body. I thought each day was going to be my last. . . . There just aren't any words to describe that. But generally a condemned man has only one last day. All my days were my last day. The guard who used to get me for my walk regularly announced that I was heading for the gallows. Just to joke. I don't know how I kept from going mad. This mental torture was worse than the other."

"What other?"

"Naturally, I was tortured, like all my buddies. Don't you people out in the world know that? Of course, the English press treats us like murderers because we're defending our country, but it's careful not to talk about the torturing. Well, you can let them know in your country that this fellow who's talking to you now was tortured. When I was arrested, I was beaten with a rifle butt first. Then they dragged me by my hair. They knocked my head against the wall. The skin of my head and scalp was black after that. Then they pushed slivers of wood under my nails. Yes, just like the middle ages; they used a hammer to do that. And that's not all. After that, they hanged me from the ceiling by my thumbs for two hours. See, after more than three months, you can still see the marks. I thought my shoulders would come out. I nearly passed out. I tell you all this because I know my own case best. But it's nothing at all compared to what others suffered. For example. . . ."

And Egan proceeded to cite other examples of atrocity. Each time, over here, I've met a man famous for his courage, whether great or small, he has always replied, "But I've done nothing compared to So-and-So. He's a real man!" And that's how you tell a real hero. . . .

"But still, why do they do it?"

"The same tactic of systematic terrorizing. They think they can frighten the Volunteers this way. The result is that every day there are more Volunteers, and they make sure they're not caught. Second, they need information. Take me, for example, they tortured me to find out where Mihall and his brother Patrick Brennan, the Dail representative, were. When they saw that, like the others, I'd let myself be killed first, they tried something else. They offered me 10,000 pounds and a passport to go where no one would know Mihall! That's like the old farmer when the police made him a similar proposition: 'Tell us only where he is and you'll get 20,000 pounds. That's very easy earned.' 'Yes,' replied the man, 'but it would be devilishly hard spent.'"

"Then you really like your General?"

"What a strange question! Are there really countries where they haven't heard of our Mihall? We would go anywhere with him! He doesn't know what fear is. When there's a tough job, he's always the first into action and the last to leave. When he's there, it's as if there aren't any bullets. You just aren't afraid. There's not a one of his Volunteers, not a single one, who isn't ready to die for him."

French Reporter Visits Volunteers' Training Camp

* * *

"General, I need your photograph."

"Will you give me yours?"

"Come now, it's not for me, it's for my French readers."

"Well, I'll tell you I don't have much time for photographers. But if you go into any police station in the country, you will see a superb picture of me on the wall, and they will be only too happy, I feel sure, to give you a copy."

"Oh, indeed, they're very fond of Mihall," cried a young history student (because all these I.R.A. general staffs are composed of intellectuals who've left their studies for more serious work). "They've put a price on his head: 10,000 pounds to the man who brings him in, dead or alive. And if they catch him, themselves, they've sworn to roast him alive."

"Why are you laughing, Gertie?" Mihall asked the pretty daughter of the house who came in carrying a package.

"Here, be good enough to eat these cakes. Can you imagine, as I was leaving the bakery, a policeman on the other side of the road, threw a pebble at me and pointed to my package, 'Is that for Mihall?' He didn't know how right he was."

Everyone laughed. Although these Volunteers are surrounded by romantic legends, they're not dark heroes. There's always a bit of the small boy in them. But a young man just rushed into the dining room, very excited:

"Mihall, there are four policemen below. They want to know why our lanterns aren't lit and whose car that is."

"I'll go down."

Mihall's boyish face became serious.

"Come down with me," he said, "it might be amusing."

Bareheaded, unarmed in his Volunteers uniform, Mihall advanced on the lighted threshold. In the shadows, four policemen in black could be made out. Then rapid dialogue ensued, loaded with meaning.

"Whose automobile is that?"

"Mine."

"What's your name?"

"Brennan."

A pause. One could imagine the policeman blanching. His voice showed less assurance: "Patrick?"

"Mihall!"

The policeman recoiled slightly. "Do you have authorization to use a car?"

"I have the right to use this vehicle during the Truce. Besides, at this moment it's being used to transport a representative of the French press." And Mihall pointed to me.

The policeman mumbled something, and the four shadows disappeared into the night.

"There aren't many policemen who can boast of seeing you as close as that."

"Quite a few have seen me up close. But they generally weren't able to boast about it."

* * *

From Limerick we returned to X____, the mountain village above the lake, where Mihall directs operations. I was invited to a Volunteers' dance. We went into a crowded room, weakly lighted by three smoking argand lamps hung from the ceiling. A thick filter of dust made the yellow light still dimmer. One sat on barrels or on boards laid on trestles along the walls.

"Watch out, you're going to fall."

And in fact there was a large hole in the floor near the barrel where I was going to sit down.

"Did dancing do that?"

"No, throwing grenades. You can see all the windows are broken, fortunately, for it gives us a little air. It didn't take the Black and Tans long to clear out! Now we have much more pleasant work in store. . . ."

All the village girls were there in bright summer blouses. The priest, whom we had just met on the doorsill, had just made a patriotic speech recommending the brave Volunteers to them. But the girls didn't seem to need that exhortation. Everyone got in place, and the violin attacked furiously those

French Reporter Visits Volunteers' Training Camp

interesting Irish jigs and horn pipes, where groups cross and crisscross, as lightfooted and complicated as flies in the springtime. Soon the dancers became worked up, stamped the beat with their feet, so that the poor violin and its breathless, accelerating rhythm could no longer be heard. And then there was a reel danced by a girl soloist, her head rigid, her body stiff, only her feet touching the ground as quickly and lightly as fluttering wings.

Mihall didn't dance, but you could tell he was there. Everything proceeded by order—by whistles from the caller. Then there was singing while the dancers rested. For me the General requested "Soldier's Song," the Irish Marseillaise. All faces were pensive. They intoned "Soldier's Song" which is serious as a hymn, vibrant as a war chant. . . .

But we had plotted something. There was, I had learned, a very popular song about Mihall making the rounds. I asked them to sing it without warning the General. Two officers came forward, called for silence, and began.

There was a flutter of surprise and pleasure in the room. All eyes were on Mihall. The man who, they say, never loses his sang-froid with the enemy, looked quite embarrassed. He was furious. Still, he couldn't keep from being pleased at the same time, and he hid his confusion behind a newspaper like a child. I heard him grumbling next to me.

"Who in the hell had the idea of singing that? (Actually he expressed himself with much more military language.) Who was the imbecile?"

"I was."

So when I find in English newspapers those invectives against those "gangs of murderers," I see again in my mind's eye those Volunteers dancing gaily with the village girls to the sound of a violin in a smoky room. I hear their laughter. I see the grave and tender looks they give their boy general. Because I've seen those blood-thirsty ruffians who, soldiers though they may be, still prefer the joys of peace to those of war.

NOTES

1. *En Irlande. De la Guerre d'Indépendance à la Guerre civile (1914–1923)* (Paris: Flammarion, 1923).
2. *L'Ile des Bardes* (Paris: Flammarion, 1925).
3. From references to Limerick, Killaloe, waterfall, mountains, and lake, we deduce that the site was a hamlet near Lough Derg.

Irish Censorship and "The Pleasure of the Text": The "Aeolus" Episode of Joyce's *Ulysses*
By Cheryl Herr

"A few years ago," lamented AE in 1928, "an advertisement which displayed a naked baby outraged our moral guardians so that the billposters in two counties had to go out with paintpot and brushes and put trousers on that infant."[1] The immediate reason for AE's complaint against such instances of what he called "moral infantilism" was the Censorship of Publications Bill then under consideration by the Dáil and passed in 1929. It is often noted by critics of Ireland that the institution of a puritanical censorship, following as it did upon the long-sought liberation of the country from British parliamentary control, constitutes an ironic trading of political domination for a kind of intellectual enchainment.[2] It is also recognized, however, that the attitudes for acceptance of such a program had never been dormant in nineteenth- and twentieth-century Ireland. During the century preceding the liberation, along with recurrent agitation for political change, attacks on free expression came from several sources. An informal curtailment of liberty combined with English control to hamper the development of the healthy political give-and-take essential to the evolution of a free state, and either impinged on or received attention from many of Ireland's journalists, politicians, and artists. The purpose of this essay is to specify the nature and extent of Irish censorship in the late nineteenth and early twentieth centuries and to determine its relationship to that part of James Joyce's *Ulysses* which comments on the role of the artist in Ireland.

In the "Aeolus" episode, Joyce gets sophisticated play out of the political conflict, moral inertia, and censoring impulses present in Irish society. Generally, this episode and the sketch that Stephen Dedalus narrates in it have been viewed by critics as direct sociological statements about Ireland. Such critics see "Aeolus" as expressing Joyce's distress over the subservience of Ireland to England and to the Roman Catholic Church. However, a comparison of "Aeolus" with the 1905 short story "Ivy Day in the Committee Room" and with the 1912 broadside "Gas from a Burner" reveals significant differences between the earlier works and the later one in the rhetorical purposes served by references to political and religious control. The narrative strategy employed in "Ivy Day," while similar to that of "Aeolus," directly involves the reader with social issues, as does the explicitly denunciatory "Gas from a Burner." "Ivy Day" was written close to the time period of its setting, and "Gas" captures Joyce's corrosive anger at the moment of composition, but the seventh episode of *Ulysses*, on which Joyce began work fourteen years after its 1904 action-time, translates that temporal distance into an emotional freedom from ideology and opinion. Rather than taking sides politically, "Aeolus" conveys the idea that art should not only circumvent the censor wherever possible but also eschew altogether the end-oriented rhetoric of politics, even when the end sought is the alleviation of ideological oppression. In fact, the final text of "Aeolus" shows Joyce's concerns to be directed to the creation of what Roland Barthes would call a "text of pleasure." Such a text literally "desires" the engagement of the reader in sensuous signification over the involvement of the reader in some pragmatic end.[3]

This reading of "Aeolus" differs from the usual view of that episode as an evaluation of Irish rhetoric.[4] Perhaps the most recent version of this approach occurs in C. H. Peake's *James Joyce: The Citizen and the Artist*. Peake argues that Joyce sets

Irish Censorship and "The Pleasure of the Text" 143

up a contrast in "Aeolus" between noble oratory of the past and the decadence of the modern rhetoric that is best exemplified in corrupt journalistic prose.[5] While this contrast of old and new is certainly present, it serves ends other than the criticism of modern rhetoricians or even of modern consciousness. The several dimensions of dialectic in "Aeolus" demonstrate the Joycean artist's position on censorship and exemplify the problems involved in making that position clear to an early twentieth-century audience. Joyce had to accomplish the tasks of attacking rhetorical ends while using rhetorical formalities and denouncing the censor without being coerced into a damaging loss of artistic effectiveness. All of this had to be done in the seventh episode in which Stephen Dedalus and Leopold Bloom were to cross paths in the building on Prince's Street that housed the *Freeman's Journal*.

II

Despite its complex structuring of ideas, "Aeolus" has a simple line of action. The episode opens with an overview of Prince's Street. There the offices of the *Evening Telegraph* and of the *Freeman's Journal* (a major Nationalist newspaper in Joyce's day) stand across the street from the General Post Office, the center of the Easter Uprising of 1916. That the action-time of the episode is 1904 does not diminish the association of this spot with the patriotic fervor that prompted the IRB's takeover of the post office two years before Joyce began composing his newspaper chapter.[6] Into this culturally important setting Leopold Bloom comes in search of an approval from the typesetter Nannetti and from the editor Myles Crawford for the ad that he wants to sell to Alexander Keyes. Bloom enters the *Evening Telegraph* office as Ned Lambert reads to a group of gathered citizens the script of Dan Dawson's eulogy of Ireland. Present are the sponging Lenehan, Si Dedalus, and professor MacHugh. J. J.

O'Molloy joins the group in search of a loan; Myles Crawford emerges from his office; Si and Ned leave to get a drink; some newsboys cause a brief commotion; and Bloom leaves the office to seek Keyes at Mat Dillon's auction house. This disparate action comes to a focus when O'Molloy and MacHugh begin a muted political and cultural debate that continues throughout the episode and that in turn centers on their attempt to secure Stephen's approval of their attitudes and of the rhetoric they admire. The editor briefly contributes to this skirmish when, receiving from Stephen Mr. Deasy's letter on hoof-and-mouth disease, Crawford tries to interest Stephen in joining what O'Molloy calls the "pressgang." Lenehan, too, seems to court Stephen's attention by poking fun at MacHugh and by telling riddles and a limerick.

All of this verbal jousting goes on as O'Madden Burke stands by, waiting for Stephen's errand to be finished. O'Molloy, a failing lawyer, recites a rhetorical period spoken by the lawyer Seymour Bushe, thereby matching Crawford's praise of the journalist Ignatius Gallaher and his transmittal to the *New York World* of coded information about the Phoenix Park murders. Competing with O'Molloy, the scholarly but seedy MacHugh quotes part of a speech given by John F. Taylor before the historical society of Trinity College. As the remaining men take up Stephen's invitation to retire to a bar, Stephen presents his "vision" about two old women climbing to the top of Nelson's pillar. The point here is that the artist's work is set against examples of rhetoric from other professional fields to highlight contrasts in intention that are made more urgent by being considered in the midst of confusion, sycophancy, and disagreement.

The structure of "Aeolus," involving the entrances, expressions of viewpoint, and exits of persons who diversely contrast with a narratively endorsed character, is a favorite pattern of Joyce's. Shades of opinion on a problem are revealed as flawed in order to isolate a workable or ethically admirable attitude toward that issue. In *Ulysses*, the episodes "Hades," "Scylla and Charybdis," "Sirens," "Cyclops," "Oxen of the Sun," and parts of "Circe" roughly conform to

Irish Censorship and "The Pleasure of the Text" 145

this pattern, one early perfected by Joyce in "Ivy Day in the Committee Room." In that impressively economical sketch, seven characters express or demonstrate attitudes that are differing shades of the dark inertia that overcame politics in Ireland with the death of Parnell. The commendable loyalty of the canvasser Hynes to Parnell's memory, to Nationalist principles, and to the working class, marks Hynes's moral superiority to the other people who enter the committee room.[7] Yet Hynes's ideas do not triumph in any way; the political malaise of the Irish remains an untouched constant in the story, as it does in "Aeolus." In that episode, Stephen's implied differentiation of artistic concerns from the goals of legal, journalistic, occasional, comic, and Nationalist rhetoric does not work changes in other characters, nor is there any indication that Stephen's attitude could prevail in Irish political life. Further, Joyce avoids the unrealistic suggestion that art is untouched by the pessimism and pain that attended political discussion in Ireland around the turn of the century. Thus, besides a similar structure and a roughly equivalent time-setting, "Ivy Day" and "Aeolus" share an undercurrent of political melancholy, a sense of loss in power and in direction since the fall of the Chief in 1891.

Readers noting this melancholy in Joyce's work may tend to see Joyce as locked into the pessimism of the years 1902 to 1904. For example, in his study of the relations of Irish literature to Irish nationalism, Malcolm Brown states that Joyce "was passionately immersed in the Fenian and Home Rule episodes. His chief limitation as an Irish witness derives from the timing of his exile. He left Ireland in 1904 at the bottom of a dreary political downswing, and he tended to view the condition of Ireland as an infinite stasis prolonging that one miserable moment."[8] This analysis both neglects Joyce's post-1904 return trips to Ireland and takes Joyce too much at the face value of his works. As Richard Ellmann notes, even after leaving Ireland Joyce remained in touch with Irish politics, and he was interested in the Uprising and the Civil War.[9] The historical perspective from which Joyce began "Aeolus" in 1918 inevitably included the bitter patriotism of 1916 along with what Brown calls Joyce's sense of the "felt history" of "Arthur Balfour's Ireland."[10] An attitude, then, of frustration informed by a vision of possible extrication underlies "Aeolus" but is readily separable from the definition of nonrhetorical artistic values that occupies Stephen Dedalus in the newspaper office.

To understand Stephen's position correctly, the reader must determine the relation of Stephen's sketch to other examples of rhetoric in "Aeolus" and to the action of the episode, for it is in what Joyce's characters say and do that the melancholia of despair, the petty one-upmanship of failure, and the fear of censorship are revealed. In basic terms, melancholy reinforces the fear of being censured, as Joyce's characters desperately seek to soothe personal and political disappointment in a balm of sanction from their fellow Dubliners. Thus O'Molloy, MacHugh, and Lenehan seek Stephen's favor and try to impress one another, using the rhetoric of others as a means of personal aggrandizement. In contrast, Stephen tries hard to wean himself from such reliance on the words or the approval of others; when O'Molloy mentions his conversation with professor Magennis, Stephen thinks, "Speaking about me. What did he say? What did he say? What did he say about me? Don't ask."[11]

This sensitivity to praise and blame combined with a desire to placate, if not impress, his peers are two of the less pleasing characteristics of Leopold Bloom. For instance, Bloom talks briefly with Red Murray as they watch the editor, William Brayden, enter the office of the *Freeman's Journal*. Murray sees in Brayden a resemblance to "Our Saviour," and this piety is reflected in Murray's comment about Dublin Archbishop William Walsh.

—His grace phoned down twice this morning, Red Murray said gravely. . . .
A telegram boy stepped in nimbly, threw an envelope on the counter and stepped off posthaste with a word.
—*Freeman!*
Mr Bloom said slowly:
—Well, he is one of our saviours also. [118]

Bloom's pose of piety and "meek smile" are intended to fool Red Murray, yet passing through the building to see Nannetti, Bloom thinks, "But will he save the circulation?" (118). That a paper called the *Freeman* is subject to religious control, however informal, is ironic, doubly so since stifling of the legitimate press can only be detrimental to the intellectual lifeblood of a nation.

Bloom's critical stance combined with his careful avoidance of verbal conflict may be usefully compared to the minor encounter between Stephen and Crawford as Stephen narrates his sketch. When Stephen casually mentions that his two Dubliners lift their petticoats to get comfortable as they sit down, Myles Crawford cautions, "Easy all . . . no poetic licence. We're in the archdiocese here" (148). Apparently such slight comments were enough to convey to an Irish audience of Joyce's time the effect of a functioning, though not necessarily formalized, censorship of the press by the Church,[12] a censorship that contributed to the pessimism and dependency that characterize most of Joyce's Dubliners.

III

That the molding of public opinion was viewed by the Church as a responsibility is readily attested to. Thanks in part to Joyce, it is popularly known that some of the blame for Parnell's downfall rests with the Irish bishops who turned against the Chief and who thereby passed on to their flock a religious party line on Parnell, albeit one that the Joyce family did not accept. So strong was Joyce's dislike of Archbishop Walsh that he includes him in his scathing and well-known indictment of Ireland entitled "Gas from a Burner." Written in anger in 1912 on the back of his contract with Maunsel and Co., the broadside is Joyce's response to the long-delayed publication of *Dubliners* and to George Roberts's attempts to censor the stories. In fact, Roberts can be taken as the speaker in "Gas"[13] and as representative of oppressive publishers throughout Ireland:

> But I owe a duty to Ireland:
> I hold her honour in my hand,
> This lovely land that always sent
> Her writers and artists to banishment
> And in a spirit of Irish fun
> Betrayed her own leaders, one by one.
> 'Twas Irish humour, wet and dry,
> Flung quicklime into Parnell's eye;
> 'Tis Irish brains that save from doom
> The leaky barge of the Bishop of Rome
> For everyone knows the Pope can't belch
> Without the consent of Billy Walsh.[14]

A misguided sense of moral superiority, a belief that Ireland is in some sense an arbiter of religious matters, the tampering with art over some spurious notion of honor, the betrayal of patriots and intellectuals, the cultural subservience of publishers, and the rule of Ireland by outsiders—these issues angered and troubled Joyce. And the things that angered Joyce are reflected in incident upon incident recorded by historians of modern Ireland.

For example, when John O'Leary, the inspiration for much of Yeats's early interest in Irish politics, edited a newspaper called the *Irish People,* he ran into major trouble with the British government and with the Church. Malcolm Brown sums up O'Leary's story: O'Leary tried to use this "seditious" paper "to call Irishmen to arms," an attempt that "led to his arrest, trial, and conviction for treason felony," as well as to "five years in English prisons and another fifteen years in exile."[15] The O'Leary case was, of course, known to Joyce; in 1907 Joyce published an essay about O'Leary in *Il Piccolo della Sera* called "Il Fenianismo. L'Ultimo Feniano." Joyce explains the resistance of the Irish revolutionaries to both "the English political parties" and Irish "parliamentarians," a resistance expressed by the "intransigent press" in which O'Leary played a part.[16]

Joyce presents O'Leary more as a political leader betrayed by a lone betrayer than as a journalist silenced by the state, but in fact O'Leary fits both roles. The militancy of those associated with the *Irish People* antagonized and frightened the English; when they were able to procure indicting evidence against O'Leary and the IRB, they took the opportunity to destroy the office of the newspaper.[17] As Marcus Bourke states: "Every scrap of paper—stationery, account books, proofs, correspondence, manuscripts, even obviously personal letters—was seized; the very floorboards were ripped up lest anything might be overlooked. A police float was summoned from the Castle and the entire type-setting machinery was loaded on to it, removed to the Castle yard and there unceremoniously dumped in an irreparable condition." Finally, "all over the country copies of the last issue of the *Irish People* were seized and confiscated by the police . . ." (Bourke 90–91). That O'Leary's paper had called for future Irish independence did not, however surprisingly, cause the publication to be outlawed until an arrest was made possible by the government's obtaining of hard evidence about IRB sedition, but the paper inevitably was killed when the arrest occurred (Bourke 54, 84). Certainly O'Leary's ultimate defense, that whatever he was to England he was no traitor to Ireland (Bourke 106), did not rescue any of his work from being considered treasonous. Notably, the Church had anticipated such an end and had warned its members not to read the paper (Bourke 73–74, 77–82). Archbishop Cullen of Dublin even publicly "thanked the authorities for the suppression of the *Irish People*"(Bourke 94).

A much milder but equally instructive case of suppression of the press involves the Irish journalist W. P. Ryan. He strongly supported a renewal of Irish culture, both by the stimulation of interest in Gaelic matters and by the initiation of debate over contemporary problems in education, agriculture, politics, legislation, and religion. F. S. L. Lyons notes (somewhat erroneously), "For a time in the early years of the new century he ran a widely read paper, the *Irish Peasant*, until it fell foul of the Church and was obliged to close down, an episode described by Ryan himself in a novel, *The Plough and the Cross.* "[18] Ryan's account of this episode,[19] which is also presented in the introduction to his book of "review" and "reverie" entitled *The Pope's Green Island*, shows how complicated and frustrating such falling foul could be, even to the most enthusiastic Irish editor. Ryan's report of his 1905-to-1910 editorship reveals persistent old-guard clerical antagonism to the intellectual debate that Ryan tried to foster in his publication. The *Irish Peasant* was edited by Ryan for only a year before the owner of the newspaper gave up its publication in acquiescence to the censure of Cardinal Logue, a censure that followed much clerical pressure on the owner's family. Although Ryan asserts that his paper found support from "a more hopeful new order of Irish ecclesiastics," Logue, in a letter to the owner, accused the *Irish Peasant* of being "anti-Catholic" and stated his intention "to denounce it publicly and prohibit the reading of it in the archdiocese" under his control. It is worth noting, though, that after some public discussion of the case, Cardinal Logue "left the 'anti-Catholic' note," and Ryan moved the paper from Navan to Dublin. When Ryan's paper—later called the *Irish Nation*—finally folded, its demise was over financial, social, and political issues rather than religious ones, despite the fact that the paper had continued fighting with "the more rigid and formalistic clerics." Hence, while the Church did not necessarily ban objectionable publications out of hand, ecclesiastical power tended toward maintenance of conservative views and public ignorance. Ryan comments that during 1906, "There was . . . the feeling on the part of the older priests that, as a friendly young priest informed me, it [the *Irish Peasant*] was 'telling the people too much.'" Judging by the tenor of the time, a reader can accept this unsubstantiated report as at least credible. The Irish press was under attack both from a hostile foreign government and from an often equally hostile native church.

Such censorship extended quite naturally to works of art. One involved incident arose over the performance of George Bernard Shaw's one-act play, *The Shewing-Up of Blanco Posnet*. When the Lord Chamberlain denied Shaw's play a license, he provided Shaw with an excellent opportunity to publish a polemical preface with the play. Far exceeding the play's length, Shaw's preface (1910) railed against the absurdities of British theatrical licensing. Because Dublin was legally exempt from that censorship, the play was eventually produced in the Abbey Theatre, and Joyce wrote a review of it. Although Joyce characteristically objected to Shaw's sermonizing in *Blanco Posnet,* he applauded the fact that the play was put on, and he noted that it had been well received by Dubliners. That reception demonstrated at least the pragmatic innocence of Shaw's play, for the Abbey Theatre had become notorious for its demonstrations against playwrights whom the audience saw as either slandering Ireland or outraging popular morality. In fact, it could be said that for a long while one of the most interesting things about Yeats's *The Countess Cathleen* or about Synge's *In the Shadow of the Glen* and *The Playboy of the Western World* was that the plays were received with verbal or physical violence when they were initially performed by the Irish Literary Theatre and the Irish National Theatre Society. During the 1907 week-long production of *Playboy,* Lady Gregory and her players engaged in what she termed "a definite fight for freedom from mob censorship,"[20] and in *Our Irish Theatre,* she notes several instances of productions in Ireland that submitted to actual or predicted audience disapproval as a criterion for rejecting or ceasing performance of a play.

Such instances of the intrusion of public opinion as a force of censorship in the theater were reinforced by yet another source of censure, Dublin Castle. Lady Gregory's stand against the Castle's attempt to ban *Blanco Posnet* threatened to lose the Abbey its license, and yet the Castle's reason for desiring the play's banning was simply to avoid appearing to contradict the Lord Chamberlain. While informing Lady Gregory in writing that the production of Shaw's play probably violated the Abbey's patent, an official of the Lord Lieutenant attempted personally to persuade her to drop the play, citing the political awkwardness of the situation, the desire to avoid the Castle's involvement with the press (the

Irish Times had published an article entitled "Have we a Censor?"), possible criticism by Dublin aristocracy, the possible concern over the play of Archbishop Walsh, and the desire to maintain a favorable "public opinion."[21] Like the Lord Lieutenant's official, an observer of turn-of-the-century Ireland finds challenges to literary and intellectual freedom at every turn.

Thus, Irish censorship was imposed by several sources and in response to varied criteria of propriety.[22] The Roman Catholic clergy maintained objections to criticisms of religion, to sexual suggestiveness, to obscenity, and to what it regarded as immorality. The British government kept tabs on writings considered seditious (that is, on anything calling for the end to British rule in Ireland in militant rather than parliamentary fashion) and was capable of intervention even in literary affairs. These sources of censure were reinforced by self-generated censorship of the sort that Stephen experiences in "Aeolus" when Crawford automatically conforms to covert controls to avoid problems. Such internalizing of or compliance with received codes became for Joyce an especially insidious source of oppression. That a printer's objection to his work could keep *Dubliners* from being published baffled Joyce and forced him to choose between desiring that his stories be made available to the public and wanting to maintain an integrity of artistic vision that threatened to be self-defeating.

A censorship based on voluntary conformity to imposed codes was encountered not only by those engaged in literary and journalistic productions but also by political commentators. The situation of Sir Horace Plunkett, Irish parliamentarian and proponent of the Irish Agricultural Organization Society, demonstrates the frustrating conflict between the independent political thinker and a coercive public. In *Ireland in the New Century* (1904), Plunkett spoke out bluntly against what he regarded as the intolerance of the Nationalist Irish toward the friends of England and toward even the friendly critics of Ireland. Bearing in mind the responsibility of the English for Ireland's educational and economic problems, Plunkett argued for a redirection of energies away from solely the pursuit of Home Rule and toward the correction of what he saw as flaws in the Irish character: a too-ready acceptance of events as destined, a comic attitude that covered over reluctance to take charge of the future, a lack of useful education and of industry (the Protestant North of Ireland excluded), and an intolerance and factionalism that made the Irish unable to work together to achieve a common goal.[23] His indiscreet criticisms of the Irish clergy, of Irish politics, and of the Irish people in general put Plunkett at the mercy of both Nationalist critics and Irish "public opinion." For the second printing of his book, he wrote an epilogue titled "After a Year of Criticism." There Plunkett commented upon the denunciation of him by the *Freeman's Journal,* one of the organs of partisanship that Plunkett deplored as so prominent in the forming of public views, and he noted, "By the term 'public opinion' I mean that part of a people's thoughts and feelings the free expression of which is tolerated by the forces which rule in the matter. I must not be understood as implying that, in the strife and clamour of our public life, the spoken, or even the written word is always an accurate reflection of our thoughts and emotions."[24]

Leaving aside the difficulty of all people in all ages to reach accuracy of expression, Plunkett's comment circumspectly touches on the central problem that Joyce attacks in "Aeolus." The results of a censorship created by an amalgamation of English dominance, Roman Catholic dictation, and the Irish public's acquiescence to these forces, are portrayed by Joyce in the varieties of ignorance and disillusion displayed by the characters in the episode: the tolerance of a "public opinion" spawned from misinformation, an inflated esteem for fine-sounding rhetoric *per se,* an acceptance of subservience as somehow linked ineluctably to Irish spiritual superiority, and a reliance on jocosity and Guinness's to pass the time. Hence, although he scorned Unionist politics, Joyce provides an analysis of Irish problems that (probably unintentionally) aligns with Plunkett's descriptions, and such a coalescence supports at least the partial validity of the portrait. Where Plunkett's aim is practical, however—the rebuilding of Irish "morale" to foster the rapid improvement of Irish agriculture and industry, Joyce's aim is intellectual and aesthetic—the development by the reader of a clear vision of things as they are and of an attitude toward art that is critical of execution, not of ideology or supposed infringements on some public notion of propriety.

IV

In "Aeolus" Joyce investigates the interaction between public consciousness and private consciousness, between the public role and the personal censoring of public utterances. Yet Joyce's strategies in the episode *argue for* nothing, are a-rhetorical insofar as it is possible for a linguistic phenomenon to manifest the writer's indifference to using rhetoric as a tool of pragmatic persuasion.[25] This view of "Aeolus" amends the notion that *Ulysses* argues for such things as the acceptance of sexual explicitness in literature, the necessity to temper religious dogma with free thought, or the need for political liberation of the Irish. These ideas may be present in the novel but mostly as a result of the connotations and contexts that cling to or are evoked by the words Joyce uses. In fact, *Ulysses* is not a novel predicated on change—moral, connubial, social, or political—and it provides more textual pleasure than rhetorical message. Thus, "Aeolus" is a rhetoric that primarily persuades the reader to read and enjoy the text.

Those features of the chapter which have received the most critical comment—the Moses motif, the samples of rhetoric, the headlines, and Stephen's sketch—consistently contribute to a criticism both of didacticism and of censorship, indeed to the nurturing of a self-critical attitude that counterbalances and replaces the censor as a determinant of behavior and speech. While analyzing these features, a reader will find it helpful to probe the relationship between rhetorical example

Irish Censorship and "The Pleasure of the Text"

and the character of the speaker who admires the example, for it is in recognizing public statement and private consciousness as mutually creative forces that Joyce sees a way out of the double bind of imposed and self-generated censorship to which the Irish in *Ulysses* have fallen prey. Essentially, then, the problem of censorship is a problem of epistemology; right understanding of the function of objective reality in forming private consciousness can alert character and reader to the presence of imposed restrictions of experience and to ways of avoiding them.

One of the threads that Joyce uses to weave "Aeolus" together is the Moses motif. References to Moses occur, for instance, in the Bushe fragment, in the Taylor speech, and in Stephen's sketch title, as well as in Stephen's thoughts, all of which illustrate the attitudes typical of O'Molloy, MacHugh, and Stephen. For example, the passage from Seymour Bushe's defense in the Childs murder case, recited by O'Molloy, sharpens the characterization of O'Molloy that emerges from his conflict with professor MacHugh and from Bloom's sympathetic thoughts about him. Under the ironic headline, "ITALIA, MAGISTRA ARTIUM," O'Molloy explains that Bushe "spoke on the law of evidence . . . of Roman justice as contrasted with the earlier Mosaic code, the *lex talionis*. And he cited the Moses of Michelangelo in the Vatican" (139). After a pause, O'Molloy "resumed, moulding his words:"

—He said of it: *that stony effigy in frozen music, horned and terrible, of the human form divine, that eternal symbol of wisdom and prophecy which if aught that the imagination or the hand of sculptor has wrought in marble of soultransfigured and of soultransfiguring deserves to live, deserves to live.* [140]

A barrister, O'Molloy is interested not only in matters of law but also in the effective presentation of ideas. He responds to the periodic form of Bushe's phrasing as much as to the idea of art as a "soultransfiguring" revelation of the divinity that Bushe regarded as at least immanent in humanity. However, O'Molloy's sensitivity to rhetorical forms, to the similar "moulding" that both stone and language are subject to, has not kept him from professional failure. Bloom considers O'Molloy in these terms:

> Cleverest fellow at the junior bar he used to be. Decline poor chap. That hectic flush spells finis for a man. Touch and go with him. What's in the wind, I wonder. Money worry. . . .
> Practice dwindling. A mighthavebeen. Losing heart. Gambling. Debts of honour. Reaping the whirlwind. Used to get good retainers from D. and T. Fitzgerald. . . . Believe he does some literary work for the *Express* with Gabriel Conroy. Wellread fellow. [125]

Bloom foretells doom, but O'Molloy is not yet totally dispirited. He values his own analytic powers, and he therefore takes several opportunities, at first mildly and then more aggressively, to qualify the attitudes advanced by the somewhat facile MacHugh. For example, the two men spar a bit over a matter of comparative linguistics or at least over the sounds of words and their possible connotations. When Crawford, absurdly referring to the professor's teaching of Latin, calls him a "bloody old Roman empire," the lawyer comments "gently," "*Imperium Romanum*. . . . It sounds nobler than British or Brixton. The word reminds one somehow of fat in the fire" (130). Crawford pessimistically adds that he and O'Molloy—the ordinary Irishman—are "the fat in the fire" (131). In turn, MacHugh cautions that "sounds of words" may be misleading; he notes that the Romans are thought of as "imperial, imperious, imperative" but that they generated a "vile" civilization in which the construction of the "watercloset" played a major part. O'Molloy counters in a murmur that "we have also Roman law." Responding, MacHugh cites Pontius Pilate as the "prophet" of that law, a cutting remark that O'Molloy ignores as he tries to divert the conversation by telling a joke which, typical of events in this chapter, he never gets a chance to finish (131).

The entrance of Stephen and O'Madden Burke interrupts

this conflict of personalities, but when Crawford mentions politics, particularly the saving from physical harm of the Austrian Emperor Franz Joseph by an Irish "wild goose,"[26] O'Molloy and MacHugh again deliberately try to one-up and correct each other's comments. Further, O'Molloy extends this contention when he tries to defend modern lawyers against Crawford's suggestion that they are all only shadows of the likes of Whiteside, Isaac Butt, and O'Hagan. It is in defense of the modern lawyer that O'Molloy quotes Bushe, but having done so, he is concerned with the effect that the rhetorical fragment has on Stephen. Stephen's nonverbal response makes clear the emotional, though somewhat mechanical impact that the fragment has on him: "Stephen, his blood wooed by grace of language and gesture, blushed" (140). The mechanisms of blushing and of periodicity are comically joined in the language of this sentence, a fact that O'Molloy is unaware of as he asks Stephen's opinion of AE and of "the opal hush poets" (140) that O'Molloy apparently disdains.

Before Stephen answers, MacHugh breaks in to introduce his recitation of John F. Taylor's comments on the revival of the Irish language. Perhaps MacHugh's recollection was simply triggered by O'Molloy's discussion of poets associated with the Gaelic movement or by the fact that Taylor compared the Gaelic movement to the Israelites' struggling under Moses' leadership to break free of Egyptian domination and to adhere to their own language and law. However, MacHugh's manner suggests irritation with O'Molloy over his attempt to corner Stephen's attention. Thus MacHugh speaks pointedly to O'Molloy as he introduces his quotation and only then turns "slowly from J. J. O'Molloy's towards Stephen's face" (141). MacHugh's long and impressive recitation ends with an evocation of Moses' leaving the mountain with the divine commandments in his possession. O'Molloy's comment—"And yet he died without having entered the land of promise" (143)—reveals his desire to undercut the effect of MacHugh's stirring oratory. However, when Stephen suggests that all gathered go out for a drink, O'Molloy lingers to tap Crawford for a loan, and the professor immediately leads Stephen away, eagerly commenting on Stephen's own recited "vision." At the close of Stephen's story, MacHugh is delighted by Stephen's use of a title that refers to Moses. He says to O'Molloy, "We gave him that idea" (149), but the lawyer, depressed by Crawford's rejection of his request for money and worn out by the prolonged verbal tension, only "sent a weary sidelong glance towards the statue [of Nelson] and held his peace" (150).

The battle between O'Molloy and MacHugh is more temperamental than political or cultural. To O'Molloy, a man well trained and intelligent but unwilling or unable to defend his position indefinitely (not a very good characteristic for a barrister), sullen acquiescence is preferable to long-term and possibly unresolvable contention. The scholarly MacHugh is made of sturdier stuff, but he is, as Lenehan jocularly points out to Stephen in his limerick, a person who "wears goggles of ebony hue" and "mostly sees double" (134). The duplicity of MacHugh's vision is peculiar; whereas O'Molloy is simply beaten down by failure, MacHugh perversely glories in it. For instance, MacHugh sees his teaching Latin as wrong; he should, he suspects, teach the more "spiritual" Greek. Even worse, he speaks English, which he regards as the most material of languages, but he does nothing to change either situation. Thus he represents a characteristic that he sees as especially Irish, the inability to combine victory with spiritual wholeness. In fact, he regards failure and spirituality as somehow causally related. To MacHugh, Ireland's failure to secure Home Rule is self-justifying.

Not a double-seer, O'Molloy pierces through lofty ideals and empty assertions, and is bothered by MacHugh's political analysis. O'Molloy lacks the qualities of character that would enable him to follow through on what he sees correctly as useful activity or reasonable ideology. This lack of aggressiveness has combined with probable ill luck to make of O'Molloy a pessimist of the worst sort, one who is aware of his own superior insight and understanding and who, though embittered by experience, remains pathetically anxious to win acceptance from those who show critical intelligence commensurate with his own. Judgmental to a fault, O'Molloy is careful to qualify all ideas, whether his own or others'. Even when MacHugh comments on Crawford's apparent drunkenness by saying, "He's pretty well on," O'Molloy responds evasively and critically: "Seems to be, J. J. O'Molloy said, taking out a cigarette case in murmuring meditation, but it is not always as it seems" (130). And in truth, Crawford's "incipient jigs" are not a constant; at times he converses lucidly and even acutely. It is appropriate, then, that O'Molloy, who sees through appearances, is attracted to the strikingly sculpturesque form of Seymour Bushe's phrasing, which does not deceive because it does not really affirm anything. When he gave this quotation to O'Molloy, Joyce might have had in mind a comment that Yeats made in the introduction to William T. Horton's *A Book of Images,* a book Joyce owned. Yeats comments that "though one may doubt whether Allegory or Symbolism is the greater in the horns of Michael Angelo's *Moses,* one need not doubt that its symbolism has helped to awaken the modern imagination. . . ." Yeats adds that this work would have a different meaning for different "generations" because "no symbol tells all its meaning to any generation. . . ."[27] Yeats's belief in the multivalent meanings inherent in a great work of art accords with O'Molloy's tentativeness, but O'Molloy is ironically led to see through appearances only to find his own pessimism underlying all events.

This distorted outlook is matched by MacHugh's flawed sight. Lenehan's analysis of MacHugh is acute precisely because he ties together the doubleness of MacHugh's attitudes (simultaneous acceptance of failure and assertion of superiority) with the reflection of the professor's blindness in those around him. Criticizing MacHugh, Lenehan says, "*I can't see the Joe Miller. Can you?*" (134). Stephen mutely receives Lenehan's gibing mockery, but his later labeling of his own recitation as a "vision" firmly counters Lenehan's scoffing shortsightedness. In fact, Stephen's actions and thoughts show his constant attempt to maintain a constructive and clear-sighted criticism both of his art and of his experience. So firmly does independence attract Stephen that his desires are virtually apolitical, a fact that is crucial to the correct understanding of Stephen's parable.

To contrast with and therefore underscore Stephen's independent, self-critical vision, the "Aeolus" episode includes headlines that give the chapter the look of newspaper copy and that demonstrate the oversimplification, sensationalizing, and stereotyping with which the popular press shapes public opinion. Some readers have questioned whether Joyce's capitalized lines are actually headlines. Whether these phrases are viewed as headlines, subheads, or captions is not necessarily important to understanding "Aeolus,"[28] for all of these verbal phenomena conform to similar syntactic and formal requirements; they are all examples of what Heinrich Straumann calls "block language," and they exist not so much to head up chunks of copy or to stand out as emphasis as to make obvious the varieties of journalistic overstatement that daily feed a dependent and largely uncritical public opinion.[29]

Complicating this general cultural problem, Joyce suggests that the press, which could operate as a "savior" or as a villain, stands on easily assailed middle ground. On the one hand, the press is subject to strictures from Church and State, a situation probably also alluded to by the presence of headlines in "Aeolus." As Francis Phelan points out, the headlines and Bloom's thought as Red Murray cuts an ad out of the paper ("Scissors and paste" [177]) allude to Arthur Griffith's *Scissors and Paste*, a short-lived journal that pieced together headlines from various official newspapers to form ironic commentaries on current events while avoiding censorship.[30] On the other hand, the press, at least in *Ulysses*, presents as fact what is often a blown-up version of personal opinion. While the headlines in "Aeolus," as Stuart Gilbert indicated, conform roughly to the changes in headline language from the Victorian age to the early twentieth century,[31] they also reflect individual points of view. Thus, the viewpoints of people present in the *Telegraph* office are mirrored from time to time in the headlines to create comic

Irish Censorship and "The Pleasure of the Text" 161

and satiric effects.³² This strategy cleverly extends the narrative technique that Joyce used in *Dubliners* and perfected in *Ulysses*. As Hugh Kenner states in *Joyce's Voices,* Joyce liked to allow the narrative voice to move close to and adopt the verbal viewpoint of a single character being discussed or presented.³³

When we look into the headlines for this technique, we can see that using "HIS NATIVE DORIC" (126) to describe the style of Dan Dawson's overblown laudings of Irish landscape represents professor MacHugh's viewpoint; for a scholar of the classics to describe this style as "native Doric" has a mildly comic effect; it implies a criticism of Dawson's vocabulary at odds with Bloom's thought that "it goes down like hot cake that stuff" (126). Similarly, "LENEHAN'S LIMERICK" (134) pinpoints what is important in the scene to Lenehan, but does not touch Stephen's significant thoughts of Mulligan's mockery. Lenehan's curiously sycophantic self-absorption thus receives a penetrating sidethrust. "FROM THE FATHERS" (142) heads up Stephen's recollection of a passage from Saint Augustine' *Confessions* but ignores the body of the section's text that is devoted to MacHugh's recital of the Taylor speech. Finally, some of the closing headlines seem unmistakably to bear the imprint of Myles Crawford. So used to diocesan control is he that he automatically reads into Stephen's sketch mildly pornographic possibilities that would require his professional excision. "SOME COLUMN!—THAT'S WHAT WADDLER ONE SAID" (147) and "DIMINISHED DIGITS PROVE TOO TITILLATING FOR FRISKY FRUMPS. ANNE WIMBLES, FLO WANGLES—YET CAN YOU BLAME THEM?" (150) reflect Crawford's suspicions.

Hence the headlines make private reality prominent, a conclusion that may be supported by listening to the gramophone recording Joyce made in 1923 of the Taylor speech (H. M. V. Paris). Where the headline "FROM THE FATHERS" interrupts the speech, Joyce drops his voice so that the line becomes part of Stephen's thoughts on Augustine. What seems to be implied is Stephen's performing an act of mental distancing from his own experience that is basic to the artistic perspective he evolves in "Aeolus"; nonetheless, the viewpoint remains Stephen's; it does not represent the total experience being narrated and suggested. While some of the headlines appear to show the attitudes only of an impersonal narrator (possibly an embodiment of the press throughout history), others reflect the attitudes of characters present, whose own experience not surprisingly seems to them to be paramount and accurate. The situation here, of course, is one that Joyce's narrative strategies often illustrate, that objective reality and subjective experience subtly interfuse to make each individual's perception not only different from that of everyone else but also less than whole.

Stephen's thoughts about and verbal response to the Mosaic motif in the works quoted by O'Molloy and MacHugh make the same point that the headlines do. Stephen's immediate recognition in contrasting the two recitations is that MacHugh's quotation presents Moses differently from the Bushe excerpt. In contrast to Bushe's evocation of a sculpture of Moses, Taylor refers to Moses as a young man listening to an Egyptian priest extol Egyptian culture. Having heard part of Taylor's oration, Stephen thinks, "Noble words coming. Look out. Could you try your hand at it yourself?" (142). To belie that possibility, Stephen's thoughts emerge in fragments:

> Nile.
> Child, man, effigy.
> By the Nilebank the babemaries kneel, cradle of bulrushes: a man supple in combat: stonehorned, stonebearded, heart of stone. [142]

In Stephen's quick associations, preceded by a minimal Ignatian composition of place ("Nile"), Moses is imagined at three points in his life: as the child rescued from the river's edge, as the competitive youth who rescued an Israelite slave by murdering an Egyptian, and as the stone figure in the Michelangelo sculpture. These three stages represent the

Irish Censorship and "The Pleasure of the Text" 163

processes of aging and of definition that Moses underwent in his own life and as a cultural figure. Stephen's recorded thoughts do not put forward any argumentative point. Rather, the reader is left to draw the commonsense conclusion that any single vision of Moses gives a distorted sense of Moses' life and cultural significance. Stephen's attempt at triple perspective, though still limited, at least avoids the single-mindedness of the headlines.

The attempt to compensate for limitations of knowledge and conception is furthered in Stephen's reported sketch. Early in the episode Crawford asked Stephen to write some copy for him in "the lexicon of youth," "Something with a bite in it" (135). Stephen responds with a short narrative about two old women. He describes in some detail the routine life led by Florence MacCabe and Anne Kearns, and their climbing up Nelson's pillar. At the top of the monument, they consume brawn, bread, and plums, and spit the plumstones through the railings. This sketch, often compared with Joyce's stories in *Dubliners*, appears to be a simple and noncommittal rendering of Dublin life in 1904 as it might be experienced by two women who lack husbands, education, and money.

Stephen's portrayal of the women is selective as well as naturalistically descriptive. When he mentions that the two women live in Fumbally's lane, he is able to move outside of his structured narrative to tell MacHugh that the lane is "Off Blackpitts," but that concentration on place leads Stephen to other thoughts that he does not weave into his narrative: "Damp night reeking of hungry dough. Against the wall. Face glistening tallow under her fustian shawl. Frantic hearts. Akasic records. Quicker, darlint!" (145). From these details the reader can assume that Stephen witnessed a sexual encounter that showed a side of "DEAR DIRTY DUBLIN" (145) that would definitely find no place in the daily news. On the other hand, the "Akasic records" of all thoughts and words, eternally existent, necessarily include this visceral side of Irish experience, but Stephen chooses to present a story that is more common than censorable. The reader has to question whether or not Stephen has thereby submitted to a mental censorship that is just another version of the internalized authoritative dictates that shaped public consciousness in Stephen's city. It seems clear, though, that Stephen's thoughts are not suppressed because of an attempt to avoid condemnation; rather, Stephen includes only those details that contribute to his story functionally, his chief aim being to achieve a convincing specificity. That Stephen captures a wholeness that resists reductivist interpretation may be attested to by surveying some of the meanings that have been attributed to the sketch and by comparing them with the interpretation that MacHugh finds in the story both before and after Stephen manufactures a title for him.

The sketch has come in for a lot of critical interpretation. Richard Ellmann, for instance, has seen it as a portrayal of Dublin as the "Promised Land" turned a waste land of "bondage" in which Stephen refuses to serve.[34] More recently, Ellmann states that in the parable Stephen "savagely mocks both British glories and Irish chauvinism."[35] William York Tindall, finding in an "indefinite" but suggestive "epiphany," sees one focus to be the oppression of Church and State which results in infertility and "subjection" for the Irish.[36] Stuart Gilbert calls the sketch an "ironic fable,"[37] while Clive Hart labels the story "a picture of futility and sterility" and links the old women with Moses and their plum-eating with escapism,[38] a position with which Stanley Sultan basically agrees.[39] Finally, M. J. C. Hodgart regards the women as "the two phases of Woman that preside over birth and death," so that the "Mosaic reference suggests that they are the midwives of the New Ireland, and the layers-out of its stillborn corpse."[40] The consensus is that the story denounces the sexual, political, and religious condition of Ireland and obliquely expresses Stephen's disgust or dismay at this condition.

A good deal of textual evidence exists to support this reading, but much of it is based on a too-selective consideration of Joyce's use in the chapter of several motifs arranged as oppositions. Awareness of this selectivity can be cultivated by following in the text the contrast between mechanism and organicism. At the beginning of the chapter, trams, mailcars, and printing presses dominate the mechanized "HEART OF THE HIBERNIAN METROPOLIS" (116). Doors creak, barrels thud, presses thump. "Machines," thinks Bloom, "Smash a man to atoms if they got him caught. Rule the world today" (118). These thoughts coincide with Bloom's idea that Dignam's death was the result of a mechanical malfunction. In "Hades" Bloom had likened the heart to a pump that "gets bunged up and there you are" (105). Bloom further reflects that the machinery of Dignam's body is "out of hand" but still "Working away" (118) to ferment itself to nothingness. Further, Bloom sees that the printing presses radically affect the lives of the typesetters. Nannetti, the foreman, moves and speaks somewhat mechanically. "Iron nerves," thinks Bloom as he struggles to communicate to the foreman Alexander Keyes's idea for an ad (120) while the machines dominate the scene with their incessant noise. However, this domination is countered by Bloom's tendency to humanize the mechanical processes he witnesses. Thus the backward setting of type reminds him of his father's reading of the Haggadah at Passover, a detail that reinforces the Mosaic imagery in the episode. And Bloom sees the press itself as "Almost human. . . . Doing its level best to speak" (121), an assertion that is especially comic in the light of the headlines that appear in "Aeolus." The organic or human seems to exist not as a contradiction but as a function of mechanism, both incidental offshoots of vast processes of generation and decay.

Sharing the dominance of the machine in the opening pages of the chapter are images of royalty and England. The central street in the episode's opening is Prince's street, and Edward VII's mailcars bear the royal insignia, while Nelson presides over Dublin's heart. However, the posited relationship between Britain and Ireland is not just that of political domination and servitude, for Professor MacHugh extends the opposition into the historical realm and poses the spiritual orientation of Judaism, Greece, and Ireland against the

"Material domination" (133) of Roman and English culture. Questioning where spirituality shows up in conquering Britain, MacHugh sneers, "Lord Jesus! Lord Salisbury" (133). The Lord of the Christian church is contrasted with the leader of the Conservative Party in England, the uncle of Arthur Balfour, and the man whom Joyce, in his essay "The Home Rule Comet" (1910), quoted as saying, "Let the Irish stew in their own juice."[41] Yet existing side by side with the conquering forces of Britain and mechanization is an undercurrent of "LIFE ON THE RAW" (145), the ordinary life of Dublin. The king's insignia is on the mailcars, but Irish shoeshiners are under the post office porch. Irish laborers transfer barrels of Guinness's from warehouse to wagon. And Davy Stephens, the famous Irish vendor, appears as the first explicit "mockery of victory"[42] in the chapter when he is referred to as a "king's courier" (116). The men of or around the press are occupied with quite ordinary and quite Irish details of day-to-day life, even though they work in the midst of royal emblems and a not-so-free press. Even Bloom contrasts the official governmental news in the *Dublin Gazette* with "ads and side features" (118) that not only account for sales of a newspaper but also are "More Irish than the Irish" (119).

"Aeolus" thus includes a series of contrasting motifs, including Latin/Greek, English/Irish, Egyptian/Hebrew, royal/common, death/life, monument/man, matter/spirit, ephemera/Akasa, frustration/creation, factionalism/humanism, law/justice, success/failure, and domination/servitude. These contraries tend to pit a stultifying mechanism against a vitalizing organicism but only in the sense that decay is necessary for growth and opposition for resolution.

Thus, although these oppositions suggest that choices must be made and offensive elements eliminated, it is clear that the episode is less concerned with weeding-out than with careful discrimination. Even the end of the episode does not dictate the blanket choice of one set of terms over another. It has been observed that after Stephen's recitation of his sketch, the true paralysis of Ireland is symbolized by the short-circuited trams, Ireland's heart being out of touch with its body.[43] This observation fails to take account, though, of the ever-present undercurrent of ordinary activity recorded in "Aeolus." Even though the trams are "becalmed" (149), other sources of transportation continue to function as "Hackney cars, cabs, delivery waggons, mail-vans, private broughams, aerated mineral water floats with rattling crates of bottles, rattled, lolled, horsedrawn, rapidly" (149). The ultimate mockery of England's mechanical and material domination is the continuation of common Irish life suggested by the functioning of "horsedrawn" conveyances that do not rely on the electric power source of the trams. The raw side of Dublin, from which Florence MacCabe and Anne Kearns emerge, is not especially spiritual, but neither is it mechanical. Dublin is the source of Stephen's art and the point at which contraries coexist; to portray it accurately the artist must avoid one-sidedness, overschematization, and oversimplification.

The artist must also avoid the argumentative ends that the political orator would seek to achieve and that some critics see as the primary intent of Stephen's story, mostly, one would imagine, because of Stephen's title for the sketch. MacHugh, in response to Crawford's question about the name of Stephen's piece, suggests that they call it *"deus nobis haec otia fecit,"* but Stephen responds with a dual title: *"A Pisgah Sight of Palestine or the Parable of the Plums"* (149). As O'Molloy points out, Moses "died without having entered the land of promise" (143); hence Sultan speaks for many readers when he maintains that the old women are similarly frustrated viewers of an Ireland that does not achieve its true promise. Of course, Stephen's sketch is also subject to the *caveat* of Myles Crawford. The sexual innuendo that Crawford senses when the women lift their petticoats to sit down is enhanced by the reading embodied in the headlines to Stephen's narrative, where the sketch is misrepresented as sexually suggestive. Some readers, following the lead of these distorting headlines, have seen in Stephen's portrayal the frustration of elderly virgins climbing the symbolic phallus of Nelson's pillar.

However, given the care with which Joyce has dissociated often distorted individual viewpoints from a full vision of reality, it seems apparent that in the sketch political commentary and sexual innuendo, like all of the details and allusions present, contribute to a story that is principally about human inadequacy. Like the *Dubliners* stories, Stephen's narrative deals with human limitations and with problems of adaptation to inhibiting external conditions, issues in which politics and censorable activities enter not centrally but obliquely.[44] The story of Anne Kearns and Florence MacCabe shows their process of pursuing knowledge of their city and understanding of their place in it. The two women are "vestals" (145); they lack, in addition to intellectual sophistication and broad cultural experience, sexual knowledge. Their trip exercises in them several emotions and brings them to a meager measure of new emotional and factual knowledge. They feel fear, amazement, hunger, giddiness, fatigue, and thirst. Even the physical fact of the pillar's height surprises them: "Glory be to God. They had no idea it was that high" (145).

To go beyond seeing the sketch as a portrait of limitation tempered by small pleasures is to grab at the sop that Stephen flings ironically to MacHugh and the rest of his audience. The title Stephen proposes leads a reader directly into an interpretation of the sketch as a work of doctrinal argumentation, however debatable the point, rather than one of selective description. It is to see the sketch as does MacHugh, who attempts to formulate a reading even before he has heard the whole of Stephen's short recitation. For MacHugh the two women with umbrellas are the "Wise virgins" (145) of Christ's parable. The fact that Florence "takes a crubeen and a bottle of double X for supper every Saturday" while Anne uses "Lourdes water" on her lumbago (145) MacHugh mechanically classifies as "Antithesis" (146). He is delighted by Stephen's use of the historically allusive phrase "onehandled adulterer" (148), and he follows up the recitation with the statement that Stephen's bitterness is like that of Antisthenes. (Stephen's objection to this comparison shows up in "Wandering Rocks" when he thinks of the "brainsick words of sophists: Antisthenes" [242] and in "Circe" where he warns Zoe to "beware Antisthenes, the dog sage" [523].) MacHugh then takes credit for giving Stephen the idea for the Mosaic slant to the title. Such unfocused attempts at analysis tell us more about MacHugh than about Stephen or his story; they fit well the character whose eyes are "Witless shellfish" while he recites a speech about right vision; and they show the aesthetic danger that Irish art was especially susceptible to. As Yeats knew, the Irish artist had to resist becoming the servant of nationalistic purposes in order to retain independent vision.[45] Certainly, any artist has to avoid being controlled by the kind of audience whose incomplete, mechanical, and delimiting analysis would border on a form of censorship.

Stephen's narrative is a response, then, to the goal-oriented uses of language in the various professions and a challenge to the interpretive powers of his audience. It is also a rejection of the mechanism that he detects even in his own self-expressive and self-involved poetry. Stephen severely criticizes the stanza he composed on Sandymount Strand, a stanza reworked from part of Douglas Hyde's translation of an Irish poem:[46]

> *On swift sail flaming*
> *From storm and south*
> *He comes, pale vampire,*
> *Mouth to my mouth.*

[132]

When Crawford tries to enlist Stephen's services in journalism, simultaneously casting scorn on current pressmen and orators, the editor's mouth twitches "in nervous curls of disdain." Stephen thinks, "Would anyone wish that mouth for her kiss? How do you know? Why did you write it then?"

(138). Further, he asks himself, "Is the mouth south someway? Or the south a mouth?" (138). Not only does his poem fail to express a reality that could include Myles Crawford's mouth as a form of the possible, but the rhymes in the poem seem to Stephen to have neither organic justification nor beauty.[47] They are two identical men: "mouth south: tomb womb" (138); the first set of rhymes, he implies, has no more meaning than "tomb womb," a rhyme he apparently considered but discarded on the strand (48). In fact, Stephen's rhymes have no more content value than the editor's "Ohio"—a possibly nonsensical interjection but also what MacHugh calls a "Perfect cretic" (127). Stephen appreciates the possibilities of poetic language only when a master like Dante uses rhymes so expressive that the words seem to become animated to correspond to the reality they suggest; Stephen thinks of the colorful poetry in which Dante describes three "approaching girls." In contrast, he sees his own rhymes as more like Dantesque "old men," not vivid but "leadenfooted" and "underdarkneath the night" (138).[48] Stephen's analysis, though subjective, displays his discontent with the formalities of poetry as he has used them.

Stephen seeks an art that either uses mechanical forms to create an engaging richness or reflects ordinary life in detail. By these criteria, his sketch is far superior to his poem, for the poem lacks beauty while the sketch has the saving grace of accuracy. The two old women Stephen saw on the beach, the fruit vendor working at the foot of Nelson's pillar, and the churches of Dublin contribute to Stephen's narrative the specificity of the actual. The fact of Irish subservience to religious and political forces is suggested in the sketch because of Stephen's reliance on Dublin as the source of his material, not because Stephen seeks to blend into his art issues that will one day be as much "Dead noise" (143) as the speeches Daniel O'Connor made at his "monster meetings," or the rhetoric of Taylor and Bushe, or the journalistic exploits of Ignatius Gallaher.

Irish Censorship and "The Pleasure of the Text"

V

As Stephen recognizes, issue-bound rhetoric is appreciated after the fact mostly in terms of formal effectiveness. Ultimately, the effect on Stephen and his companions of the best rhetoric they hear in "Aeolus" is to please them, and their pleasure comes as much from a relishing of form as from the workings of nostalgia. Certainly the average reader of *Ulysses* appreciates "Aeolus," if at all, because the episode demands that we make some fairly fine discriminations among characters and uses of language, bids for laughs in the changing relationship of headline to text, and makes witty and self-conscious use of rhetorical tropes. The pleasurable effects of such a demanding reading experience have been analyzed by Roland Barthes in *The Pleasure of the Text*. Barthes attempts to describe the relationship between the reader and a work that gives the reader pleasure. He claims that such a text actually desires a reader who will desire the text; reader and text enjoy each other, an experience that sometimes intensifies to moments of climax that Barthes calls "blissful." An application to *Ulysses* of Barthes's textual "erotics"[49] is necessarily fragmentary and focused on those points on which Barthes's criticism and Joyce's art appear to converge. Nonetheless, those points reveal both something of the wide applicability of Barthes's theories and the virtual hedonism of *Ulysses*.

For example, Barthes defines for us the *"clivage"* between textual pleasure and textual bliss:

> Text of pleasure: the text that contents, fills, grants euphoria; the text that comes from culture and does not break with it, is linked to a *comfortable* practice of reading. Text of bliss: the text that imposes a state of loss, the text that discomforts (perhaps to the point of a certain boredom), unsettles the reader's historical, cultural, psychological assumptions, the consistency of his tastes, values, memories, brings to a crisis his relation with language. [Barthes 14]

Barthes's sense of continuity between the reader's relationship with culture and the reader's "relation with language" finds confirmation in Joyce's blending of the political issues of censorship and oppression with delight in form that goes, as far as possible, beyond the argumentative. In this light, the headlines may be seen as devices that short-circuit a reader's possible empathy with the oppressed and frustrated Dubliners of 1904. Political and social ironies become less deadly when teamed with a comic device that partially disengages a reader from the issues referred to in the text.

The interplay of culture and reader comes up again when Barthes discusses what he calls *"Mandarinat"*:

> All socio-ideological analyses agree on the *deceptive* nature of literature (which deprives them of a certain pertinence): the work is finally always written by a socially disappointed or powerless group, beyond the battle because of its historical, economic, political situation; literature is the expression of this disappointment. These analyses forget (which is only normal, since they are hermeneutics based on the exclusive search for the signified) the formidable underside of writing: bliss: bliss which can erupt, across the centuries, out of certain texts that were nonetheless written to the glory of the dreariest, of the most sinister philosophy. [Barthes 39]

The pertinence of this quotation to "Aeolus" is striking, for many readers accept as Joyce's and Stephen's primary aim the denunciation of oppression and frustration in Ireland; yet such a reading misses the nonpragmatic function of Joyce's verbal play. Such readers may have difficulty accounting for Joyce's textual gymnastics and may even recur to Joyce's charts of *Ulysses* to "explain" the presence of rhetorical tropes and headlines in "Aeolus."

Barthes associates "bliss" with "rapture," with "wisdom," with "significance," with "avant-garde" literature, and with the ineffable (Barthes 19, 25, 38, 20, 21). Any of these things can instigate in a reader the response Stephen has to Dante's brilliant verse. Much of the pleasure that Barthes finds seems contingent on a text's not being delimited by a single meaning, as well as by the text's having a signification that is more sensuous than intellectually definable. For instance, when Barthes proposes a *"Society of the Friends of the Text,"* he states that

> its members would have nothing in common (for there is no necessary agreement on the texts of pleasure) but their enemies: fools of all kinds, who decree foreclosure of the text and of its pleasure, either by cultural conformism or by intransigent rationalism (suspecting a "mystique" of literature) or by political moralism or by criticism of the signifier or by stupid pragmatism or by snide vacuity or by destruction of the discourse, loss of verbal desire. Such a society would have no site, could function only in total atopia; yet it would be a kind of phalanstery, for in it contradictions would be acknowledged (and the risks of ideological imposture thereby restricted), difference would be observed, and conflict rendered insignificant (being unproductive of pleasure). [Barthes 14–15]

Thus, the enemies of this society would include the people to whom Stephen narrates his sketch in "Aeolus," for Crawford, MacHugh, O'Molloy, and Lenehan all share in various ways in a strident narrow-mindedness. Their single visions make them indifferent to or unable to appreciate the multivalence of art. Similarly, they would be puzzled or possibly outraged by Joyce's own attempts to create pleasure by the nonaffirmation of any of the contraries formed by the episode's motifs, by seeking third terms that contribute to the continued existence of contraries in a larger and more completely rendered reality (Barthes 54–55). In Joyce, opposition often exists unresolved and unresolvable; even the tension of political insecurity is maintained in a state of unrest that can contribute to the reader's pleasurable excitement.

Rhetoric itself, as argumentation, as persuasion, or as formality, is not disparaged in the episode; its very omnipresence demonstrates that rhetoric cannot be avoided when language is the medium of expression. Yet the text affirms as an ultimate good the potentiality of the reader's pleasure, even of his bliss. Joyce's extensive use of the rhetorical trope in "Aeolus" lends support to the notion that the text is a site of pleasure, for it is in the fulfillment of an anticipated pattern that an audience often finds excitement and satisfaction. Following Stuart Gilbert, Don Gifford and Robert J. Seidman have listed over one hundred figures of speech in "Aeolus," from the pun (which Richard Ellmann finds to be the source of "a constant small excitement" in Joyce's works[50]) to hapax legomenon.[51] Discussing Joyce's revisions of "Aeolus," Michael Groden states:

> Tropes were on Joyce's mind during his early work on "Aeolus," as notebook VIII.A.5 clearly indicates. Of the ninety-five rhetorical devices Stuart Gilbert lists for the episode, sixty-four were included by the time of the fair copy. . . . Joyce's late desire for all-inclusiveness increased his audacity in the examples of rhetorical devices; nevertheless, he filled the episode with devices from the start.[52]

Further, Groden points to Joyce's exuberant "last stage" addition of "startling, unique phrases" to the text.[53]

Such extensive and insistent use of formal conventions has ordinarily been read as Joyce's criticism of overt verbal mechanism and of instruments like the press that rely on stock linguistic forms. However, even the minimal humor of a phrase like Lenehan's "Muchibus thankibus" (140) tends to deflate such a pretentious aim and to reveal Joyce's apparent delight in repetition, rhythm, neology, and word manipulation not bound to meaning. Like the headlines, phrases like "Clamn dever" and "Madam, I'm Adam" (137) cause ripples in the textual surface that may momentarily engage a reader in the same primitive pleasure that characterizes an audience's response to the often disjunct patter of the stand-up comedian, to the gestures and falls of the slapstick comic, and to the predictable order of repetitious popular melodies and lyrics, as well as to the crescendo and release of a well-delivered speech, be it political or dramatic.

It is worth stressing the fact that simple recognition of linguistic forms that predict their own completion creates pleasure for the reader on a level that is partly separable from meaning. An antithesis with chiasmus, such as Stephen's "Poor Penelope. Penelope Rich" (149), does not necessarily carry any thematic meaning. However, several "explanations" of Stephen's thought could be invented (cf. Barthes 34), and the search for a meaning can provide the pleasures of pursuit, of rendezvous, and of consummation between reader and text. Joyce constantly weaves literary conventions, linguistic forms, and social phenomena together in passages that can vibrate into meaning but need not be overread. To make verbal experience more varied, intense, and challenging is to heighten the reader's involvement in the text and to enhance the noetic enjoyment of seeing "the Joe Miller."

A case in point is the narrator's description of MacHugh's tone, when the professor begins introducing the Taylor quotation, as "ferial" (141). Given the sound of the word and MacHugh's apparent irritation with O'Molloy, one might read the unusual *ferial* as having overtones of ferocity. Did Joyce have in mind rather *feral*, a word that comes from the Latin *fera* (wild animal) and connotes brutality and atavistic savagery? In archaic usage, *feral* also means "deadly," "funereal," or "gloomy,"[54] suggestions that would neatly fit in with MacHugh's description of the sickly Taylor, who "looked (though he was not) a dying man" (141). To check this possibility, the reader might consult the Rosenbach Manuscript, but there Joyce clearly wrote *ferial*, a word that remained unchanged in the *Little Review* version of "Aeolus" and in the 1922 Paris edition of *Ulysses*.[55] Recalling MacHugh's exhortation that we not be led astray by the sound of words, the reader might instead note that *ferial* refers to a day on which no ecclesiastical feast is celebrated. What sort of tone, then, is a "ferial tone"? One that is simply nonfestive? Perhaps, but such play with possibilities of sound and meaning serves to make Bloomsday, in fact, a feast-day, or at least an occasion for pleasure.

NOTES

1. AE, "The Censorship in Ireland," *Nation and Athenaeum* 44 (22 December 1928): 435–36; rptd. in *The First Freedom: Liberty and Justice in the World of Books and Reading*, ed. Robert B. Downs (Chicago: American Library Association, 1960), p. 391.

2. See, for example, Francis Hackett, "A Muzzle Made in Ireland," *Dublin Magazine*, n.s. 11 (October-December 1936): 12–13; rptd. in *First Freedom*, p. 395.

3. Roland Barthes, *The Pleasure of the Text*, trans. Richard Miller, with Note on the Text by Richard Howard (New York: Hill and Wang, 1975), pp. 6, 14–15, 65. Subsequent references will be indicated parenthetically in the text by "Barthes" and the page number(s).

4. A notable exception to the usual emphasis on rhetoric is Stanley Sultan's section on "Aeolus" in *The Argument of "Ulysses"* (Columbus, Ohio: Ohio State University Press, 1964), pp. 109–18. Sultan maintains, "The major subject of the chapter is the political character of the Irish nation" (p. 109).

5. C. H. Peake, *James Joyce: The Citizen and the Artist* (Stanford, Calif.: Stanford University Press, 1977), pp. 194–95.

6. For dates concerning Joyce's composition of "Aeolus," see Michael Groden, *"Ulysses" in Progress* (Princeton, N.J.: Princeton University Press, 1977), pp. 68–69. On the G. P. O., see Sultan, *The Argument of "Ulysses"*, p. 110.

7. Warren Beck, *Joyce's "Dubliners": Substance, Vision, and Art* (Durham, N.C.: Duke University Press, 1969), pp. 237–58, especially 242–53.

8. Malcolm Brown, *The Politics of Irish Literature: From Thomas Davis to W. B. Yeats* (Seattle, Wash.: University of Washington Press, 1972), p. 17.

9. On Joyce's mixed feelings during and after the 1916 Uprising, see Richard Ellmann, *James Joyce* (New York: Oxford University Press, 1959), pp. 411–12 and 547; cf. pp. 246–49, 267, 276.

10. Brown, *Politics of Irish Literature*, p. 17.

11. James Joyce, *Ulysses* (New York: Random House, 1961), p.140. Subsequent references are included parenthetically in the text.

12. In reference to Joyce's spending time in 1909 at the *Evening Telegraph* offices, Ellmann in *James Joyce* (p. 297) states: "The publisher of the *Freeman's Journal* was Thomas Sexton, a Parnellite who was feuding with Archbishop Walsh; consequently his paper minimized whatever the Archbishop did and enlarged upon everything that Cardinal Logue did. Walsh evidently made frequent protests, which Joyce referred to without explanation in the sentence in *Ulysses*, 'His grace phoned down twice this morning.'" The lack of explanation contributes to the generalized sense of clerical intervention in the workings of the press that Joyce cultivated in *Ulysses*. Probably a third reference in "Aeolus" to Church censorship occurs in the section headed "NOTED CHURCHMAN AN OCCASIONAL CONTRIBUTOR" (121).

13. According to Ellmann in *James Joyce* (p. 346, 348–49), "Gas" was "ostensibly spoken by Roberts himself," but blended with John Falconer, the printer who refused Joyce the printed sheets of *Dubliners*. "Gas" was printed in Trieste and distributed in Dublin by Charles Joyce.

14. James Joyce, "Gas from a Burner," in *The Critical Writings of James Joyce*, ed. Ellsworth Mason and Richard Ellmann (London: Faber and Faber, 1959), p. 243 (ll. 13–24).

15. Brown, *Politics of Irish Literature*, pp. 7–8.

16. James Joyce, "Fenianism: The Last Fenian," in *Critical Writings*, p. 188 (translation of "Il Fenianismo. L'Ultimo Feniano," *Il Piccolo della Sera*, 22 March 1907).

17. Marcus Bourke, in *John O'Leary: A Study in Irish Separatism* (Athens, Ga.: University of Georgia Press, 1967), p. 95, states that the entry and seizing of the *Irish People* office was illegal and that T. Clarke Luby, the paper's proprietor, briefly attempted to lodge a suit against "the Lord Lieutenant, the Under-Secretary and the Chief Magistrate for Dublin" (see also pp. 90, 94). Subsequent references will be indicated parenthetically in the text by "Bourke" and the page number(s).

18. F. S. L. Lyons, *Ireland Since the Famine* (London: Weidenfeld and Nicolson, 1971), p. 235n.

19. Quotations below in this paragraph are from W. P. Ryan, *The Pope's Green Island* (London: Nisbet, 1912), pp. 1, 9, 11, and 14.

20. Lady Gregory, *Our Irish Theatre: A Chapter of Autobiography* (New York: Putnam, 1913), p. 115.

21. Ibid., pp. 145–47.

22. In a 17 August 1911 letter to the press, Joyce summarizes his awareness of the several sources capable of attacking authors. Granting Maunsel & Co. the right to publish an expurgated "Ivy Day," Joyce says, "Their attitude as an Irish publishing firm may be judged by Irish public opinion. I, as a writer, protest against the systems (legal, social and ceremonious) which have brought me to this pass." See *Letters of James Joyce*, ed. Richard Ellmann (New York: Viking Press, 1966), 2: 293.

23. Plunkett summarizes these views in his epilogue to *Ireland in the New Century: With an Epilogue in Answer to Some Critics*, 3d ed. (London: Murray, 1905).

24. Ibid., p. 297 (see pp. 298–99).

25. A similar argument, involving Joyce's attempt in *Finnegans Wake* to transcend language, occurs in Margot C. Norris, "The Consequence of Deconstruction: A Technical Perspective of Joyce's *Finnegans Wake*," *ELH* 41 (Spring 1974): 130–48.

26. Don Gifford with Robert J. Seidman, *Notes for Joyce: An Annotation of James Joyce's "Ulysses"* (New York: E. P. Dutton, 1974), p. 109 (131: 20–22—131: 23).

27. William T. Horton, *A Book of Images*, With an Introduction by W. B. Yeats (London: Unicorn, 1898), p. 9. The fact that Joyce owned this book is cited in John J. Slocum and Herbert Cahoon, comps., *A Bibliography of James Joyce 1882–1941* (New Haven, Conn.: Yale University Press, 1953), p. 176.

28. For useful discussion of the headlines, see Marilyn French, *The Book as World: James Joyce's "Ulysses"* (Cambridge, Mass.: Harvard University Press, 1976), pp. 98–101. She argues that in the seventh episode "No one position is unambivalently right, no perspective can contain the whole," and that the headlines, which "function in various ways," "compound the contradictions of the episode" (p. 98).

29. Heinrich Straumann, *Newspaper Headlines: A Study in Linguistic Method* (London: Allen and Unwin, 1935), pp. 38–39; when Straumann explains the term *block language*, he mentions that the language of Joyce's *Work in Progress* has similarities to it. Straumann argues for "the existence of headlinese as a language, a jargon, a dialect, or whatever it may be called, of its own," and he cites "sociological, psychological, grammatical, and historical evidence to prove this assumption" (p. 25). He discusses the distorting powers of headlines that do more than provide "a

simple label" over the story in question (p. 26) and notes, "Supposing there is such a thing as public opinion influenced by the Press, this influence must largely go by way of the headline . . ." (p. 27).

30. Francis Phelan, "A Source for the Headlines of 'Aeolus'?", *James Joyce Quarterly* 9 (Fall 1971): 146–51.

31. Stuart Gilbert, *James Joyce's "Ulysses"*, 2d ed. (London: Faber and Faber, 1930), p. 174, n. 1.

32. Cf. Peake, *James Joyce: The Citizen and the Artist*, p. 195.

33. Hugh Kenner, *Joyce's Voices* (Berkeley, Los Angeles, London: University of California Press, 1978), pp. 16–17, 21. Similarly, Erwin R. Steinberg contends in *The Stream of Consciousness and Beyond in "Ulysses"* (Pittsburgh, Pa.: University of Pittsburgh Press, 1973), p. 112, that the narrator in the early Stephen-dominated episodes of *Ulysses* sometimes adopts Stephen's idiom even in omniscient narration.

34. Richard Ellmann, *Ulysses on the Liffey* (New York: Oxford University Press, 1972), pp. 70–71.

35. Ellmann, *The Consciousness of Joyce* (Toronto and New York: Oxford University Press, 1977), p. 81 (see also pp. 38, 53).

36. William York Tindall, *A Reader's Guide to James Joyce* (New York: Noonday-Farrar, 1959), p. 166.

37. Gilbert, *James Joyce's "Ulysses"*, p. 178.

38. Clive Hart, *James Joyce's "Ulysses"* (Sydney, Australia: Sydney University Press, 1968), p. 53.

39. Sultan, *The Argument of "Ulysses"*, pp. 114–15. Sultan also emphasizes the political theme of the parable (pp. 115–17).

40. M. J. C. Hodgart, "Aeolus," in *James Joyce's "Ulysses": Critical Essays*, ed. Clive Hart and David Hayman (Berkeley, Los Angeles, London: University of California, 1974), p. 126. Overall, though, Hodgart gives the sketch an odd but more hopeful twist: "The midwives have presided over the birth of a miraculous Child, and now a great Modern writer is among us" (p. 126).

41. James Joyce, "The Home Rule Comet," in *Critical Writings*, pp. 210, 213 (translation of "'La Cometa dell' 'Home Rule,'" *Il Piccolo della Sera*, 22 December 1910).

42. The "sense" or "meaning" of "Aeolus" according to the scheme Joyce gave to Carlo Linati.

43. Sultan, *The Argument of "Ulysses"*, p. 117; Hodgart, "Aeolus," in *James Joyce's "Ulysses": Critical Essays*, p. 119.

44. On the "realism" of Stephen's sketch, see Frank Budgen, *James Joyce and the Making of "Ulysses"* (London, Oxford, Melbourne: Oxford University Press, 1972), p. 99, and Peake, *James Joyce: The Citizen and the Artist*, pp. 196–99.

45. Lyons, in *Ireland Since the Famine*, pp. 233–42, discusses the resistance of Yeats and of John Eglinton to patriotic pressures.

46. Weldon Thornton, *Allusions in "Ulysses": An Annotated List* (Chapel Hill, N.C.: University of North Carolina Press, 1961), p. 62 (48.3).

47. Cf. French, *The Book as World*, p. 95. Hugh Kenner notes in *Dublin's Joyce* (London: Chatto and Windus, 1955), p. 251, that "Joyce always sets Romantic poetry in close touch with mechanism."

48. For the Dante references, see Gifford/Seidman, *Notes for Joyce*, p. 113 (136: 37—137: 7–8).

49. Richard Howard speaks of Barthes's book as defining an *"erotics of reading"* (Barthes viii).

50. Ellmann, *The Consciousness of Joyce*, p. 90.
51. Gifford/Seidman, *Notes for Joyce*, pp. 519–25.
52. Groden, *"Ulysses" in Progress*, pp. 92–93.
53. Ibid., p. 105.
54. The *OED* cites these meanings of *feral*; the entries under both *feral* and *ferial* suggest some historical confusion of the two words.
55. Clive Driver, annot., *James Joyce: "Ulysses": The Manuscript and First Printings Compared* (New York: Octagon-Farrar; Philadelphia: Rosenbach Foundation, 1975).

DATE DUE

DEMCO 38-297